S
95

THE CRESTLINE SERIES

MODERN U.S. MILITARY VEHICLES

Fred W. Crismon

MBI Publishing Company

DEDICATION

*To the grandkids: David Taylor Crismon
and Rowan Gayle Schaefer*

First published in 1998 by MBI Publishing Company, 729 Prospect
Avenue, PO Box 1, Osceola, WI 54020-0001 USA

MBI Publishing Company books are also available at
discounts in bulk quantity for industrial or sales-promotional use. For
details write to Special Sales Manager at Motorbooks International
Wholesalers & Distributors, 729 Prospect Avenue,
Osceola, WI 54020-0001 USA.

Library of Congress Cataloging-in-Publication Data
Crismon, Fred.
     Modern U.S. military vehicles/Fred W. Crismon.
          p. cm.--(Crestline series)
     Includes index.
     ISBN 0-7603-0526-9 (pbk.: alk. paper)
     1. Vehicles, Military--United States. I. Title. II. Series.
UG618.C72   1998
623.7'47'0973--dc21 98-19124

On the front cover, top left: A competitor for the Army's light tank
program was the XM8 Armored Gun System (AGS), once known as the
CCVL. Built originally by FMC (now known as United Defense), this
vehicle is also still on the market, and is designated as the M8 AGS. The
outward appearance has changed somewhat, but it still retains most
characteristics of the initial model—a 52,000-pound gross weight, driven
by Detroit Diesel's Model 6V92TIA with 580 horsepower from 552
cubic inches. The transmission is a hydromechanical Lockheed-Martin
HMPT 500-3EC which incorporates hydrostatic steering and multidisc
oil-cooled brakes, and a final drive ratio of 4.4:1. Torsion bars provide
the suspension, and a flat track is used. *MFG*

On the front cover, top right: The first Oshkosh Palletized Loading
System (PLS) trucks entered service in the fall of 1992. With five driving
axles and two steering axles up front, it has a GVW of 88,000 pounds,
with the truck being at least 50,000 pounds of that (or 55,000 if it is
equipped with a Grove self-loading crane). The overall length is 36 feet,
on a 224-inch wheelbase. The pallet lifting system is a Multilift Mk V
derived from the French Bennes Marrel system, and it has a loaded
pallet ready to place on the ground in this view. *MFG*

On the front cover, bottom left: The GAU-12/U 25-millimeter Gatling
Gun is also known as the Vulcan, and the name is appropriate for a
weapon that can spit out 2,200 25-millimeter (1-inch diameter) bullets
per minute, so fast that the sound is a deafening burp. That is 36
rounds per second. The weapon is preferred for anti-aircraft roles, and is
equally effective against softer targets. The Standard Manufacturing
Company of Dallas, Texas, used their practical little 8x8 Trailing Arm
Drive chassis as the mount for the Gatling Gun, using hydrostatic drive
and braking and a GVW of 16,000 pounds. Ground clearance varied
from 10 to 22 inches, and the top speed was 45 miles per hour using a
Detroit Diesel 6.2-liter V-8 with 135 horsepower. *AF*

On the front cover, bottom right: This is the station wagon of the
HMMWV line. An armored superstructure with a taller roof line, hump-
backed rear section, and external stowage of individual gear indicate
that this is the troop carrier. Ten fully equipped troops can fit into this
rig, if a lot of their gear is hung outside. A .50 caliber machine gun is
secured to a pedestal mount; the gunner would stand on the
transmission tunnel. There is no M-series number for this
configuration, as it has not been adopted by the U.S. military. *MFG*

On the back cover, top: General Dynamics and MAN GHH of Germany
have teamed up to build this Wolverine heavy assault bridge (HAB). It is
to be the replacement for the aging AVLB which is based on the M60
series medium tank. It differs from the earlier types in that they were a
scissors design (hinged in the middle), while the Wolverine uses an
auxiliary diesel engine to first slide the lower section out, then the
second section drops and is coupled to the first section, and the entire
85-foot bridge assembly is moved out to the front without touching the
ground until it is ready to emplace. The aluminum bridge weighs 12
tons, while the complete vehicle is 70 tons. It can launch a bridge in five
minutes, and retrieve one in 10 minutes. Based on a M1 tank chassis, it
uses the normal AGT-1500 engine and a X1100 transmission. *MFG*

On the back cover, bottom: The Oshkosh M1070 prototypes were ready
for testing in the fall of 1990, with production set for spring 1992. Over
1,500 have been built, all using Detroit Diesel's 8V-92TA, which
developed 500 horsepower, working with an Allison five-speed
transmission, and the Oshkosh 55000 series two-speed transfer. All
axles were Rockwell Model SVI 5MR series, with planetary reduction
gears out in the hub and differential locks on the tridem, with the first
and fourth axles steering. The huge cab will carry five fully equipped
troops, helping to bring the GVW to 87,000 pounds. The curb weight
was 41,000 pounds. An M88A1 tank retriever is on the trailer in this
view.

Printed in the United States of America

CONTENTS

ACKNOWLEDGMENTS

As with *U.S. Military Wheeled Vehicles and U.S. Military Tracked Vehicles*, the assistance given by individuals, corporations and government agencies has been quickly forthcoming and greatly appreciated. Special thanks go to Joe Fogle (Manning Equipment), Tom Griffin (Century Wreckers), Craig MacNab (AM General), Jim McMillan (Caterpillar), John Sobczyk (TECOM), Col. Gary Steimer and Maj. Scot Hagan (TEXCOM), and Mike Thomas (Chenowth).

Photo credits are noted by initials following the caption. Where no initials are present, the photograph was taken by the author.

Photo Credits. AD-Alain Dailloux; AEB-Armor & Engineer Board, Ft Knox, KY; AF-U.S. Air Force; AFCC-U.S. Air Force Combat Camera; AFJ-Armed Forces Journal; APG-Aberdeen Proving Ground, MD; ARMY-U.S. Army; BK-Benno Knorr; CC-Clark Culbertson; CK-Carl Kaelble Archives; DAVA-Defense Audio Visual Agency; DP-Deorr Peterson; EAST-Maj. Bob East; EC-Ernie Cooper; EK-Eliott Kahn; ET-Etnyre Archives; FAUN-Faun Archives; FB-Fort Belvoir, VA; FE-Fontaine Equipment; FPM-Ford Photo Media; FWD-FWD Archives; GP-Government Publication; GS-Glenn Sokolofsky; HDT-Hayes Diversified Technologies; HM-Heil Manufacturing Archives; JA-Jim Atkinson; JAL-Jim Allen; JM-Jacques Mermaz; JMB-Jean-Michel Boniface; JS-John Sobczyk; KF-Kaffenbarger Company; LETA-LeTourneau Archives; ME-Manning Equipment; METZ-Metz Archives; MFG-Manufacturer; NA-National Archives; NAEC-Naval Air Engineering Center, Lakehurst, NJ; NASM-National Air & Space Museum; OGE-O'Gara Hess & Eisenhardt; QMC-Quartermaster Corps; RIA-Rock Island Arsenal; RP-Robert Peot; RVO-Ramstein Vehicle Opns; RW-Richard Wright; SS-Stars & Stripes, Darmstadt, GE; TAC-Tank-Automotive Command; TS-Tim Schwalbe; USMC-U.S. Marine Corps Archives; VPC-Vehicle Processing Center, Mainz, GE; VV-Bart Vanderveen; WES-Waterways Experiment Station; WT-Wheels & Tracks.

The United States military owns and operates perhaps the most varied collection of automotive vehicles to be found anywhere in the world. Between the Army, Navy, Air Force, and Coast Guard, there are vehicles that traverse snow, sand, mud, swamp, paved roads, and any other type of surface one can imagine. They range in size from tiny four-wheelers and dune buggies to immense amphibious Hovercraft. Furthermore, these vehicles are utilized by military elements that are stationed on nearly every continent on the earth.

Trying to keep tabs on such a far-flung and diverse fleet of motorized equipment is impossible. Part of the problem is that much of the equipment is procured locally in foreign countries, and the only way to know about it would be to frequently visit the country where the equipment is used. Another problem is that some of the equipment, although built in the United States, is generally not in the public view.

During World War II, any new tank was considered classified, and they were often referred to as new "secret weapons." These attitudes of security prevailed well into the 1950s, but began to disappear as the public wanted to know more about the equipment, and as it became obvious there was no need to classify their very existence. The thickness and composition of armor is still classified in most cases, but the technical details of all of America's combat equipment is now generally available to the public. Indeed, the manufacturers now even print advertising material, something that was unheard of in World War II.

Of course, most of the military's motorized equipment is in the form of standard cars and trucks, and these are often simply civilian models put to administrative military use. But other vehicles are often very unique. The Air Force and Navy both require aircraft loading and servicing vehicles and runway snow plows. The Army has trucks that can be reduced in height for air drop operations. And all of the services require specialized fire and emergency vehicles.

Several of the armed services have specialized branches: the Navy has the Seabees, the SEALs, and the Marines. The Army has its Special Forces, and the Air Force also has special operations units, along with a combat engineer element known as Red Horse. These unique branches often have missions that require strange and unique motor vehicles. The Army's Special Forces and the Navy's SEALs both utilized high-powered dune buggies during Desert Storm for high speed reconnaissance missions. The Navy has a small fleet of huge 4x4 pickup trucks that tow inflatable boats used in shore protection operations. Perhaps less exciting, but just as important, the Navy and Air Force combat engineer units operate heavy equipment that one would not normally associate with a military unit, but they are necessary for quick preparation of runways, beaches and other surfaces for movement of supplies and equipment.

The compilation of photographs and data on U.S. military motor vehicles requires the assistance of hundreds of people from dozens of sources. Military test agencies, the using military units, contractors, military archives, photo labs, the Air Force's Combat Camera elements, and, of course, the manufacturers of the equipment have all been tapped in this effort, and without exception, all have responded with enthusiasm.

This has been an ongoing effort on the part of the author, who published *U.S. Military Wheeled Vehicles* in 1983, and *U.S. Military Tracked Vehicles* in 1992. New equipment is constantly being evaluated and procured, which requires steady attention on the part of the researcher. This volume will pick up where the previous volumes left off. It is not intended to be totally comprehensive, as there are simply too many variations on many of the modern vehicles to even attempt that. However, any comments, corrections, or suggestions may be forwarded to the author through the publisher.

CHAPTER ONE

A HISTORICAL REVIEW

The very first motorized vehicles purchased by the U.S. military were bought in 1899. There was a roadster and two light trucks, and all three had been built by the Woods Motor Vehicle Company of Chicago. There seems to be no record of just why these electric vehicles were purchased, but all three were quickly sent to the Philippine Islands, where the United States was engaged in the Spanish-American War, to serve with the troops "in the field."

Over the next 14 or 15 years, small numbers of electric, steam, and gasoline vehicles were added to the government's military fleet. Apparently, they were mostly purchased in ones and twos, and seem to have served essentially as signal dispatch cars, light delivery vehicles, or as officers' cars. As late as 1912, the popular automobile magazine *Motor Age* reported that the military owned only 20 trucks.

A cross-country expedition involving five trucks was sponsored by the U.S. Army in 1912. Two of the trucks finished the 1,500-mile trip from Washington, D.C. to Indianapolis (by way of Atlanta), in only 45 days. Despite the horrible or nonexistent roads, the trip proved that trucks could go "cross-country" and deliver the goods. Army maneuvers at Plattsburg, New York, in July 1912 employed numerous trucks loaned by companies and private individuals, and this also helped to convince Army authorities that the "motor" was here to stay. By the end of 1914, the U.S. Army alone owned 80 trucks and 35 passenger cars. The number of vehicles owned by the U.S. Navy at that time is unknown.

When the U.S. Army began its incursions into Mexico in 1916 to search for Pancho Villa, it became obvious that horses were not the answer to the transportation problems south of the border. Trucks and cars were soon employed in this effort, which involved long trips deep into the hostile interior of Mexico. By April 1916, about 370 trucks were in the military inventory, with more than 300 of these on the Mexican border with General John J. Pershing. Several dozen of these trucks utilized a new and unusual concept that delivered power to all wheels: four-wheel drive.

Despite the increased numbers of vehicles, there was obviously not much organization behind the purchase of these trucks and cars, and by the time the punitive expedition into Mexico was over, there were at least 128 different makes and models in the fleet. This lack of standardization may have pleased a lot of small manufacturers, as they could state (and most of them did) that the government had bought a few of its products. But it created a nightmare for anyone trying to find repair parts or trying to train repairmen. Plus, many of those 128 types were not very good vehicles. The worst, however, was yet to come.

World War I was to be the turning point in how the U.S. military procured its equipment. In their book *How America Went to War*, authors Crowell and Wilson claim that there were at least 294 different makes and models in the service of the American elements of the Allied Expeditionary Force in France. Of these, 213 were built in the United States, while the remaining 81 were British, French, or others.

This Knox 1/2-ton truck, circa 1904, was representative of many of the motor vehicles owned by the military in the early 1900s. Assigned to the Army's Rock Island Arsenal in Illinois, it had an air-cooled opposed two-cylinder gasoline engine of 16 horsepower, a two-speed planetary transmission, and chain drive. Creature comforts consisted of the hat, overcoat and gloves worn by the driver. *RIA*

America entered the war in April 1917, and in July of that year announced that it planned to purchase 10,550 trucks and 500 motorcycles for the war effort. This represented an immense increase over the 1,050 trucks purchased in 1916. Finally, some order also began to appear in the procurement program. Dismayed by the diversity and varying quality of so many makes and models, a plan was initiated to standardize most of the motor trucks as Standard AA (3/4 ton) Standard A (1 1/2 ton) and Standard B (3 to 5 tons), with each of these types built to identical technical and appearance standards.

By the time of the armistice in 1918, the Standard B was in full production, with a total of 9,452 identical trucks with "USA" cast into their radiator top tanks having been built by 15 different manufacturers. The 3/4-ton Standard AA never went into production, as a light GMC model had been selected to serve instead. Likewise, a White 1-1/2-ton became the "Standard A" truck.

Military tracked vehicles built by American companies by the end of the Great War consisted of only three types of very light tanks: two built by Ford and the third an improved copy of the French Renault tank. Only a few of the Ford tanks were completed, and none saw combat. The Renault replica, known in the United States as the M1917, was to have been built in 4,400 examples; however, only 64 had been completed at the time of the armistice, and the contract was canceled at that point. A few prototype tracked carriers based on British designs were also built for the Great War, but it is unlikely that any saw service in France.

The years between World Wars I and II were a relatively fertile period for both tracked and wheeled vehicle development within the U.S. War Department. It had become obvious that tanks had some special capabilities during warfare, and several Army agencies set about to develop bigger and better vehicles. More powerful engines, better cooling systems, improved track and suspensions,

By the beginning of the first World War, the Army had begun to specialize some of its motorized fleet. This c. 1916 Ford was fitted with a custom body enabling it to serve as a maintenance contact truck for Artillery units. Known as an Ordnance Repair Truck, it kept its tools and equipment under a snug-fitting cover, but left the operators out in the cold. *RIA*

more precise steering, and better creature comforts were soon incorporated into larger and more spacious tanks. There were also self-propelled artillery and tracked and half-tracked cargo carriers, and several specialized vehicles such as flame throwers and wireless (radio) receiver-transmitter rigs.

The development of wheeled vehicles during the period of 1918 to 1941 was even more aggressive than that of tanks and self-propelled artillery. After all, military trucks of that era were not substantially different from commercial models, and the motor vehicle industry was in the midst of a sizable boom. America was becoming motorized. Horses were beginning to be used mostly for pleasure, and by now, the U.S. Army was an avid supporter of motor vehicles.

In 1920, a military motor expedition traveled 3,251 miles with 73 vehicles in 62 days from Washington, D.C. to San Francisco to test the road network across the continent. They found there were no roads in many areas, and much of what had

been built was non-negotiable in any but the best of weather. A subsequent "Good Roads" project produced not only all-weather routes for the military should they ever need them, but better daily farm-to-market and city-to-city access as well.

All-wheel-drive trucks had been the most useful wheeled vehicles available during the Mexican standoff and also the war in France, despite the fact that they had primitive drive systems and that the tires used at that time were made of solid rubber and had absolutely no tread pattern. Tire chains were available, and when the troops mounted them on all four wheels, they found these versatile trucks could extricate themselves from some rather desperate situations.

Unfortunately, the American automotive industry was not at all oriented toward building all-wheel-drive trucks, and the specialty companies such as FWD, Jeffrey, and Duplex charged a hefty price for their products. In an effort to build better and cheaper trucks, the Army in about 1928 began

When the Army was not happy with the selection and quality of all-wheel-drive offerings from the American automotive manufacturers after World War I, they began to build their own. Known as the "Standard Fleet," they ranged from 1 1/4 to 10 tons capacity, and included this classy 2 1/2-ton 6x6. Only three of this model were built, one with a Duesenberg Model J engine, one with a model AED Lycoming, and one with a Franklin air-cooled V-12. Not surprisingly, they could achieve 70 to 80 miles per hour. *DAVA*

Although more than 200 of the Standard Fleet trucks were put into service, the huge majority of American military trucks between the wars were commercial models such as this 1935 Dodge. It has been equipped with over-sized General Jumbo tires for better flotation on soft soils, a brushguard to protect the radiator and headlamps, and a "conestoga" body. Fortunately, the canvas has been removed, and we can see the radio set used by Company E of the 67th Infantry (Tanks). *NA*

to produce a limited number of both rear-wheel drive and all-wheel-drive trucks in the Quartermaster shops at Fort Holabird, Maryland. They built 4x2, 4x4, 6x4 and 6x6 configurations, with tonnage capacities ranging from 1 1/4 to 10 tons, and employing the best components available on the market at the time. They called them the "Standard Fleet."

Between 1928 and 1932, the Army built more than 200 of these excellent Standard Fleet trucks, and sent them to troop units throughout the country to be put into daily use. Thus, it was no surprise when the automotive industry suddenly became interested in the project, and their lobbying in Washington, D.C. led to the Army being directed to stop making trucks. The upshot was that

numerous American truck manufacturers were soon developing and building all-wheel-drive trucks, many of which would meet the exacting standards for military service. In fact, World War II was successfully fought using trucks, which, for the most part, were modified civilian models. Even more impressive, thousands of these World War II vehicles were still running at the end of the twentieth century.

World War II was a period of frenetic activity in all areas of manufacturing in this country. Not only motor vehicles, but aircraft, ships, weapons, ammunition, medical supplies, clothing, packaged foods, and everything else one can imagine were produced in huge quantities, and carefully managed by the federal government. Rationing in the civilian marketplace was routine, and included not only critical food items, but motor vehicles, gasoline, batteries, oil, and tires as well.

There was some standardization of trucks during World War II. Both Ford and Willys built nearly identical 1/4-ton 4x4 Jeeps, and Studebaker and Reo produced identical 2 1/2-tonners. Larger models, which were standardized, included the H-542 series 5-ton 4x2, which was built by International Harvester, Kenworth, and Marmon-Herrington, and the larger 6-ton 6x6, which was built in various editions by White, Corbitt, Brockway, Ward La France, and FWD. However, most of the trucks and automobiles used during World War II were not standardized at all, but were simply militarized commercial designs. And sometimes the militarization consisted only of olive paint and special exterior lights.

New categories of motor vehicles were created during World War II. There were huge mobile cranes for lifting damaged aircraft, both on land and on the new aircraft carriers. Wheeled scrapers were built to level off terrain to make runways, and they could do it much faster than a bulldozer. The wide use of aircraft by the Army Air Corps and the Navy meant new aircraft ground support equipment had to be designed to meet maintenance and towing needs.

The development of armored vehicles, both wheeled and tracked, during World War II was even more remarkable than the progress in trucks. Early American armament was badly outgunned by German equipment, and eventually the war was won not so much by the Allies having better equipment than the Axis forces, but by overwhelming them with sheer numbers. Not only did America have immense production capabilities, but it also helped that the factories were not being bombed on a regular basis.

It wasn't that the tanks, artillery, and armored cars didn't improve during this period. Engines,

World War II brought numerous specialized vehicles into the American military fleet, and some of the most unique were found on aircraft carriers. This modified Ford 8N tractor was used by the Navy, and was known as the Moto-Tug. Built in two models with 2,500 or 4,000 pounds drawbar pull, they were designed to shuttle aircraft on the carriers. About 500 were built, all using Ford's 119-ci four-cylinder engine, three-speed transmission, 6.00x20 rear tires, and a 6.66:1 rear drive ratio. *FPM*

drive trains, track and suspension systems, and even the manner in which the hulls were manufactured all showed state-of-the-art developments, and this resulted in equipment that could withstand infinitely more punishment than their predecessors.

At the end of World War II, military planners were not as naive as their counterparts had been at the end of the Great War. Although greatly improved tanks had been fielded just prior to the end of the war in Europe, and highly efficient self-propelled artillery was now the norm, there were serious expenditures of time, talent, and money in the late 1940s to ensure that the United States would never again be caught napping if hostilities should again break out, or at least that there would always be highly capable equipment available for use.

The new truck fleet, which the Army proposed in about 1947, was designed from the ground up to satisfy military requirements. Of course, tanks and artillery have always been purely military items, designed by engineers from the ground up specifically for military use, with price considerations generally taking a back seat to reliability and durability. To justify the great cost of building trucks to meet their exacting standards, the Ordnance Corps even began to infer that the vehicles, which had served so well from 1941 to 1945, could have done a lot better had they not just been converted civilian models. There is no doubt that the new fleet of trucks was impressive, especially from the parts interchangeability point of view.

The new series had only two basic 4x4 models, the 1/4 ton and the 3/4 ton, whereas there had been numerous 4x4s during the war, ranging from 1/4-ton capacity to 6 tons. The most obvious change, however, was in the 6x6 middle weight range, from 2 1/2 to 5 tons capacity. The new 2 1/2-ton 6x6 was a squared-off design with no frills, and the entire range had the same appearance except for the body bolted to the rear of the frame. It would be built by only two manufacturers, Reo and Studebaker. The 5-ton 6x6 was quite similar in appearance to the smaller 2 1/2 tonner, but everything was somewhat larger. These 5-ton models were built by International Harvester, Diamond T, and Mack. The flagship of this new tactical truck fleet was the Mack 10-ton 6x6,

which could be found as a tractor or as a cargo truck, and it was proportionally even larger than the 5-ton models.

The presence of thousands of Americans in West Germany in the years following World War II created a huge logistics system, which depended primarily on roadways. Since most of the mechanics employed by the Americans were local Germans, it made sense to purchase equipment with which they were familiar, and repair parts would be more easily available as well. The German vehicles bought were primarily cargo trucks, busses, and fire trucks, and they created an entirely new category of motor vehicles for the Americans. The practice eventually spread to England, France and Italy as well, and motor vehicles built in these countries were routinely found in the American fleet well into the 1970s. Occasionally they were even especially engineered to meet U.S. requirements.

There were other vehicles that appeared in the years after World War II that defied the norms, and some of them turned out to be very useful. The military has always had problems moving large quantities of supplies over soft terrain, and to meet these needs, a new type of forklift was designed for the Army that could move across uneven terrain. The rough terrain forklift is still with us today, and has now been joined by an even more versatile rig, the extended-reach rough terrain forklift. Terra tires were also featured on some very unique vehicles, enabling them to traverse even soft snow, drifting sand, or mud. And although the giant FWD Terracruzers have gone to the scrap yard, the very low pressure tires are still present on some highly specialized vehicles.

The Army, of course, has not been the only service that has needed specialized vehicles. The Air Force has always required esoteric aircraft tugs, deicers, bucket lifts, runway snowplows, and missile transporter/launchers. The Navy also has some unusual missions, and carrier-based crash cranes, aircraft servicing trucks, and tugs are built to their exacting standards, while the Navy's Seabees and arctic operations occasionally get some of the most unusual vehicles of all. Happily for people writing on this subject, there will always be a need for some highly specialized piece of motorized equipment in the U.S. military.

In the 1980s, due primarily to the cost factor, but also due to the long lead times required to put exclusive military models into production, the U.S. military again began to purchase modified "off-the-shelf" trucks (Commercial Utility Cargo Vehicle or CUCV) for the tactical fleet. Although they have served relatively well, specialized tactical trucks often can be more easily modified to suit the needs of the specific mission than can a commercial model, and more durability can be designed in from the beginning.

The recent need to operate in desert areas has encouraged trucks that are even more specialized than the tactical fleet of the 1950s. The most unusual is the Fast Attack Vehicle, a dune buggy that got publicity during Operation Desert Storm. The more familiar High Mobility Multipurpose Wheeled Vehicle (HMMWV, or Hummer) is as militarily pure as one can get in a truck, and it has been modified to serve in numerous roles. Some of the largest new trucks in the U.S. military fleet such as the 8x8 Heavy Expanded Mobility Tactical Truck (HEMTT), 10x10 PLS trucks and the giant Heavy Equipment Transporter (HET) are also designed from the ground up as tactical military vehicles.

There were two major recent world events that had a curious side effect regarding the U.S. Army's military vehicle fleet. One was the fall of East Germany, and the second was Operation Desert Storm. The army of East Germany had a large quantity of tactical wheeled and tracked vehicles that were no longer needed or wanted by the new German government. When the American military forces went into Saudi Arabia for Operation Desert Shield (later known as Desert Storm) and needed equipment quickly to support these maneuvers, several thousand of these trucks and tractors of East German, Soviet, and Czech manufacture were offered to the United States for free.

Several hundred vehicles were accepted, ranging from light vans to heavy 8x8 tank transporters, and including tracked tractors and other construction equipment. These items were quickly taken to the port of Bremerhaven, and put on ships bound for Saudi Arabia. Many of them served quite well in Desert Storm, with the advantage that if they were damaged, they could just be abandoned. After their use in Desert Storm, most of the surviving vehicles were handed over to the indigenous forces for their use, but some of the better equipment was returned to Germany. When the Americans were subsequently involved in mutual reduction of missile and tactical forces in Western Europe, hundreds of these remaining vehicles, some of which had been originally built in the Soviet Union, were destroyed as part of the mutual efforts in reducing the tactical military equipment fleets, thereby avoiding the need to destroy good U.S. equipment.

The story of the East Bloc vehicles did not end there, however. The very best of the equipment that came into the hands of the U.S. military after the collapse of East Germany was brought to the United States, where it still serves today to train U.S. soldiers. Photographs of a few examples of these East German, Soviet, and Czech vehicles that served with the American military are included in this book.

Although much of the new U.S. tactical vehicle inventory was designed specifically as military equipment, the new Family of Medium Tactical Vehicles (FMTV) from Stewart & Stevenson are based on commercial designs, although of Austrian origins. The FMTV will eventually replace the 2 1/2-ton and 5-ton 6x6 trucks now in the fleet, and these new trucks are just now being issued to units in the field.

Although there were efforts in the early 1990s to include a new light tank in the inventory, that project never reached fruition. Instead, the versatile vehicles known as the Bradley Armored Fighting Vehicle (AFV) is filling the need, along with some leftover 1960's aluminum tanks known as the M551 Sheridan. Other tracked vehicle types have seen marked improvements. The M1 Abrams medium tank (now referred to as a Main Battle Tank) is the only true tank in the fleet. It has been consistently upgraded and is regarded as one of the best vehicles of its type extant. Tracked self-propelled artillery, missile launchers, and reconnaissance and logistics vehicles have all been newly developed or substantially improved in the last 15 years.

Except for the turbine-powered M1 series tanks, everything in the American military wheeled fleet from medium trucks on up, and all of the tracked vehicles, are powered by diesel engines.

If your airfield was really remote, you got one of these Chevrolet 1 1/2-ton 4x4 models with a 500-gallon tank, PTO-driven pump (from the truck engine), and huge Firestone 14.00x24 tires with a special tread pattern. Also built around 1943 for the Army Air Corps, it had the standard 83-horsepower 235-ci six-cylinder Chevrolet engine, but offered far better mobility with its large tires and 16 inches of ground clearance under the differentials. *HM*

Even by current standards, some of the trucks built during World War II were quite large. This type of 20-ton Federal model 604 was normally fitted with a fifth wheel for towing trailers, however the unusually severe conditions found in the building of the new Alcan Highway dictated that this 1,600-gallon Heil three-compartment tank be mounted on a very heavy truck, and the Federal got the job. It had a 167-inch wheelbase, and 10.00x20 tires all around, and an 80-gallons-per-minute pump driven from the truck's PTO. *HM*

Although it took several decades to convince the U.S. military of their efficiency and durability, diesels are finally here to stay, and automatic transmissions are routinely found in even the heaviest wheeled or tracked vehicles. For ease in moving between surfaced roads and soft terrain, most of the tactical wheeled vehicles now have adjustable tire inflation systems.

One of the most notable recent changes in the management of the military's motor vehicle fleet is the involvement of the General Services Agency. For decades, the GSA purchased supplies and equipment for all government agencies, saving millions of dollars in the process, along with standardizing much of what was purchased. Around 1985, the GSA began to also manage the military's commercial vehicle fleet, operating it in much the same way a private car rental company might. They bought vehicles in huge numbers at reduced prices, operated them with careful maintenance for 50,000 or so miles, and then sold them at government auctions before they became worn out. It works quite well and keeps modern equipment in the fleet at minimal cost. But in most cases it means there are no longer U.S. Army, or U.S. Navy or U.S. Air Force markings on the driver's door. Instead, these vehicles carry a "GSA" license plate, which does not distinguish which service is operating them.

An entirely new category of motor vehicle was created to quickly move disabled aircraft on carriers. Although earlier models were quite basic, by 1945, the LeTourneau company was building this model C-202, which had 18.00x24 tires on the crane, 14.00x24 on the model C-5 Tournapull power unit, and a Continental M-271 gasoline engine with four-speed transmission driving only the front wheels. The C-202 is seen here in its stowage mode, with the crane retracted and the power unit swiveled around under the frame to save space. *LETA*

This cab-over-engine fire truck was custom built in 1952 in the American style for the U.S. Army's Corps of Engineers by Metz using a Krupp Sudwerke chassis. The German designation is Type LF 20, and featured an American layout for the pump controls and body configuration. It carried 800 liters of water, 366 meters of hose, and ground ladders. The engine was a 110-horsepower Sudwerke coupled to a five-speed transmission. *METZ*

Although built in limited numbers, this unique 5-ton 6x6 was a product of Faun Werk, Nurnberg, and was supplied to the U.S. Army around 1955 as a general cargo truck. Designated as Faun's model L908/45A, it used an air-cooled inline six-cylinder Deutz engine and a four-speed transmission. A winch was also provided, with the fairleads at the rear, probably for positioning artillery. *FAUN*

Probably the largest truck built overseas for the American forces was this Kaelble 20-ton 6x6, which was also supplied to the French and British forces in Germany. It was found in several configurations (this one has PTO-driven winches at the front and rear), but all featured an enormous gasoline V-8 engine that displaced 19 liters and produced 200 horsepower, a phenomenal figure for Europe in 1955. It had a six-speed transmission, payload of about 22 tons, and a top speed around 30 miles per hour. *CK*

This is one of the smallest and weirdest vehicles ever purchased by the American military. It was specially designed for use on aircraft carriers and was built by the O.E. Szekely Company of Philadelphia as a self-propelled electric power plant for starting Navy jets or reciprocating engines. They were built in about 1950 using a Willys Jeep as the base, but relying on front wheel drive only, with twin steering wheels at the rear mounted side by side, allowing nearly pivotal turning. Subsequent Szekely models had a more conventional wheel/steering layout. *JMB*

The LeTourneau engineers were never at a loss to find solutions to transportation problems, and when the Navy needed a powerful ground-based tug to move exceptionally heavy items, they created the Bu-Dock tractor. Built at their Longview, Texas, plant in 1954 for the Bureau of Docks, it embodied the usual LeTourneau recipe for moving things: a large diesel engine driving a large generator, with electric motors out in each of the wheels to provide the final push. Steering was by toggle switches, and the Bu-Dock tractor also had a powerful winch at the rear. *LETA*

The FWD Company of Clintonville, Wisconsin, built this utility truck around 1954, either as a potential candidate for the Army's new Jeep program, or as an offering for foreign markets. Although similar to Willys' model CJ-3B, it had a somewhat roomier body, diamond plate front fenders, and an integral Koenig front winch. The drive train was conventional with an L-head four-cylinder engine, three-speed transmission, two-speed transfer, and solid axles. The Army eventually bought the technically advanced but problematical M151. *FWD*

As military mobility became more demanding, various forms of all-terrain forklifts were experimented with. This air droppable version was known as the L-42 Sandpiper, and it had terra tires to assist in movement over sandy beaches. Developed by the Quartermaster Corps in 1962, it had a 4,000-pound capacity, and used torsion bars for articulation in roll, along with front wheels that pivoted to the rear for picking up the pallet, then pivoted forward for travel. *QMC*

In the early 1960s, the Air Force had some 8x8 FWD Terracruzer chassis to carry their Mace and Matador missiles and the ancillary support equipment. These giants were based on an updated version of Edward Albee's Rolligon principle, which replaced normal tires with large rolling air bags. This 6x6 version of the Terracruzer was built around 1960 for the Army, featuring the power plant out over the rear axle assembly, and an extendible boom forklift at the front. *JAL*

Weird and wonderful are the inventions sold to the American military, including this 5-ton cargo truck with pivoting cab. Known as Transportation Systems Incorporated (TSI) Model IS 15X, they were built in 1975 in Denton, Texas, for the huge Air Force Logistics Center at Warner-Robbins AFB, Georgia. The truck is in the travel mode in this view, with the cab out front so the driver has a good view of traffic, or at least as good as it will ever get. The idea worked, but they were a hydraulics nightmare and prone to frequent breakdowns.

Modern Wheeled Vehicles

CHAPTER TWO

MOTORCYCLES AND STAFF CARS

Although motorcycles had played a major role in the Army from the years before World War I right through World War II, they took a nosedive in the 1950s. Once a primary means of dispatching messages (World War I), and of traffic enforcement (World Wars I and II), safer and warmer methods of mobility prevailed and the motorcycle was rarely seen in U.S. military livery after about 1955. When the fuel crunch hit in the 1970s, there was a feeble attempt to put soldiers in the saddle who were simply carrying correspondence around a military post, but nobody was very serious about it. It was still safer and drier to ride in an enclosed vehicle.

There had always been an undercurrent of thought that a good cross-country motorcycle might have some true military potential, and foreign armies have used them for decades. But the U.S. military did not put them to the test until the late 1970s when motorcycles began to be used in training exercises. Numerous makes and models were tested including Honda, Husqvarna, Kawasaki, Suzuki, Yamaha, and Herkules, with Harley-Davidson eventually entering the competition.

The 9th Infantry Division at Fort Lewis, Washington, began using motorcycles in 1981 for reconnaissance chores and as message carriers, the same roles they had excelled in during the First World War. The Marine Corps had begun testing around 1977. Of course motorcycles still have the same major drawback they had in 1916: total exposure to the weather for the rider. However, they still had the advantages as well, including the ability to move with agility through rough terrain, often getting through when four-wheeled vehicles cannot.

The new lightweight bikes have a level of maneuverability and reliability only dreamed of during World War II, and the comfort factor is a bit better as well, due to better ergonomics, superior suspension systems, and the improved clothing available to riders. They can also now be ridden at night using night vision devices.

Although the Army was to have purchased 6,000 motorcycles in 1986, the funding was withdrawn in 1988 due to spending constraints and disagreements on their effectiveness. But excellent use was made of motorcycles during Desert Storm as reconnaissance vehicles as well as message carriers. They were used extensively by the Marines in courier and scout roles, and the Army's Special Operations Command even had a few of their Desert Mobility Vehicle Systems (DMVS), which is a HMMWV with an M-116A2 trailer modified to carry a Kawasaki KL-250D8.

Although there are still a variety of makes and models in service, the motorcycle of choice for both the Army's Special Operations and for the Marine Corps seems to be the Kawasaki KL-250D8, with the Marines having ordered 265 of them in 1991.

Staff cars have generally not altered their status in military usage in the last decades, with the great majority simply being a four-door sedan or a station

In December 1977, a young Marine posed with his Suzuki Model TS-185 while performing during a field exercise as a message courier. He was assigned to the Communication Company of the 9th Commo Battalion, First Marine Division. These 185-cc displacement machines were relatively light commercial machines that had been developed as cross-country sporting bikes and displayed no modifications for military use. *USMC*

wagon that just happens to belong to one of the military services, and which is sometimes painted in the preferred color of that particular service. The exceptions are that in the 1990s, they will usually be painted in whichever color was in the paint guns when they came down the assembly line.

In most cases, the Army, Navy and Air Force no longer have these administrative vehicles on their vehicle inventories, but they are the property of the government's General Services Agency. While it is cheaper to not insist they be painted in military colors,

it also has the added advantage of making them easier to sell when they have accrued 50,000 or so miles (most potential customers do not care for gloss olive), and it offers a lower visual profile in areas where it is better to remain anonymous.

The most vivid exception to the staff car picture of past years is that there is now a substantial fleet of armored sedans for the use of senior officers, a result of the turbulent times in which we live.

By the time American troops were sent to Panama in 1989 on an operation with the self-serving name of "Just Cause," military motorcycles had acquired a more purposeful look. These two Yamaha XT-350s show military lighting and extra hand and thigh protection along with the olive paint. The XT-350 costs around $3,000, which is far below the current $30,000+ cost of a HMMWV, the next cheapest vehicle in the tactical fleet. *AFCC*

The Army's Special Operations Command and the U.S. Marine Corps have settled on the Kawasaki KL-250D8 as their bike of choice. They have four-stroke, liquid-cooled engines, which means they are quieter and pollute less than a two-stroke model. Costing $3,100 each, they can reach 80 miles per gallon with their 46-tooth rear sprocket and wider-than-normal tires. These Kawasakis were modified by Hayes Diversified Technologies to meet U.S. military requirements and can carry 350 pounds including the rider. *MFG*

Although the Harley-Davidson MT-350 was available by 1991 and was technically comparable to the Kawasaki KL-250, it did cost nearly $2,000 more per machine. Due to its stronger frame and suspension, it could carry 450 pounds including the rider, but the extra weight capacity was not needed by the military. It has a 200-mile range, can ford about 20 inches of water, and has been in service with the British, Canadian, and Jordanian armies for several years. *MFG*

STAFF CARS

Terrorist threats in the 1980s led to the provision of a fleet of armor-plated staff cars for the use of senior officers. This Mercedes-Benz 380SE was one of several provided to the military in Germany, with this one assigned to 7th Army Headquarters in Heidelberg. They carried an outward appearance nearly identical to a standard Mercedes, with only the door posts and window frames having a more substantial look. At close range, the glass is also much thicker than normal. Armor plating was also retrofitted around and below the passenger compartment.

From 1991 through 1996, the General Services Agency purchased Chevrolet Corsica sedans for use by the military services, and although they are rotated out of the fleet when they reach 50,000 or so miles, there are always a large number to be seen. The traditional Air Force, Army, or Navy markings on the doors have been replaced by blue on white government license plates, while this Fort Dix, New Jersey, car also carries a Fort Dix window decal.

Despite the takeover by the GSA of the administrative vehicle fleet, there is still some random acquisition of unusual vehicles, especially outside the United States. The military in Germany still purchases Opels, German Fords, and even an occasional Volkswagen sedan, which makes them less noticeable in traffic unless they are carrying other markings as well. This 1990 Volkswagen Jetta has the license plate of the Berlin Brigade, before the demise of East Germany.

CHAPTER THREE

COMMERCIAL TRUCKS

The majority of the commercial trucks currently in service with the American armed forces are under the auspices of the General Services Administration, as are the passenger cars. They are often purchased in large quantities on a nationwide basis, and as long as the military agency that is requesting them stays within set guidelines, the truck will be identical to hundreds or thousands of others distributed to other military bases.

Although there are a wide variety of "standard" trucks to select from the "catalog," including make, model, chassis and body variations, trucks, by their very nature, often need to be custom-built to meet a specific need. Hence, most military bases will have a few quite unusual rigs that have been special-ordered, but these will usually also be managed by the GSA. As a result of the GSA involvement, commercial trucks will usually not have any Army, Navy, or Air Force markings on the doors, but will carry the ubiquitous GSA license plates instead. As with passenger cars, the colors of trucks will also be whatever is being offered by the manufacturer at the time it comes down the assembly line.

The differentiation between commercial trucks covered in this chapter and the tactical trucks in Chapter 5 can sometimes be a matter of semantics.

Tactical trucks will almost always have all wheel drive, but there are a large number of all wheel drivers in this chapter as well. The trucks described in this chapter are essentially "off the shelf" models, which are as easily available to the civilian community as to the military. On the other hand, the term "tactical trucks" will generally describe specialized military-oriented vehicles, which would not normally be offered through a commercial truck dealership.

The Russian and Eastern European vehicles that were donated to the United States by the German government for use in Desert Storm are also included in this chapter. Although they would certainly have been used as frontline tactical trucks in their native East Germany, Czechoslovakia, and the Soviet Union, they were also consistently sold around the world as commercial cargo trucks, and that is the role that the Americans gave them in Desert Storm.

It should be noted that the tonnage categories that follow are rather arbitrary. Most of the vehicles might well be able to handle more weight than indicated, especially on improved roads or when pulling a semi-trailer, but in an effort to break these vehicles out into manageable groups, approximate weight capacities were used.

Volkswagens in the service of the American forces in Germany are quite common, and new models are regularly added to the fleet. This 1988 1/4-ton Golf is actually a light van, and is used in traffic management situations in the Heidelberg community. Equipped with a 1,588-cc four-cylinder liquid-cooled diesel engine and five-speed transaxle, it is capable of about 90 miles per hour, but can also deliver close to 40 miles per gallon.

One of the most popular very light-weight 4x2 vehicles these days are the "four wheelers" or All Terrain Vehicles. When properly handled, these machines can go almost anywhere, and even have something of a flotation capability thanks to the oversized tires. This is an Air Force Honda TRX200 in use in Saudi Arabia during Desert Storm, but the Army and Navy keep some in inventory as well. The TRX200 had a 192-cc one-cylinder engine with a dual range five-speed transmission. *AFCC*

1-Ton 4x2

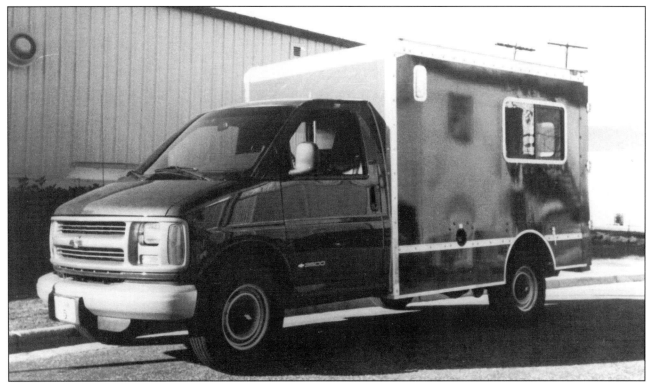

Chevrolet's G series cutaway cab and chassis was used as the basis for this Grumman-Olson "breadvan" body, which can be found on any Air Force base. Using a 1997 series 3500 chassis, it has a 5.7l V-8 with 250-horsepower and four-speed automatic transmission with overdrive. These trucks, which are not managed by GSA, are used to transport crews to aircraft and for general administrative missions.

1 1/2-Ton 4x2

The American Berlin Brigade owned this unique little tractor-trailer, which consisted of a 1984 MAN-VW Model 9-136 with a Blumhardt semi-trailer. Using a VW Type LT tilting cab, MAN placed their 90-horsepower, four-cylinder diesel engine under the seats, along with their five-speed transmission. The Germans bought for the Berlin Brigade whatever makes and models the Americans felt were most efficient for use in Berlin, and some very unusual equipment could be found there.

A typical cargo and troop carrier found on Army posts throughout the United States would be this 1990 Ford low profile F-600. Using 225/70R 19.5 tires to achieve a low loading height at the bed, it had Ford's Model 165 diesel engine and an Allison AT545 five-speed transmission. The GVW was 19,000 pounds, and Midwest built the body. It was equipped with longitudinal wooden troop seats for carrying trainees. The GSA also procures similar units on Dodge and Chevrolet chassis. *ME*

5-Ton 4x2

In 1985, the Army purchased 174 of these spotting tractors, which were designed to move semi-trailers around a marshaling yard. They were based on Ottawa's Model 50 and known to the Army as their M878A1. The GVW was 84,600 pounds, with a Detroit Diesel 6V53T engine and an Allison MT653 five-speed transmission, running on 10.00x20 tires. This one belonged to the 37th Transportation Group and was caught on film at Rhein-Main AFB, Germany.

Medium-range Macks are rarely seen in Europe, but the Air Force took this 1990 Midliner MS 200P to Germany equipped with a liquid nitrogen tank body. The Mack Midliner is actually based on a French Renault design, and the American version uses a 180-horsepower Model RVI E3-180 turbocharged six-cylinder diesel with intercooler, and a six-speed Eaton 4106B transmission.

One of the more fascinating trucks of recent years is this 1994 Ford F-800 with a pickup body. But there is more: an 8,000-pound Ramsey winch, Cummins 1060 six-cylinder diesel engine, Allison automatic transmission, air brakes, air and electric connections for a trailer, extra fuel tank, dual rear tires, and a crew cab. Four were built for the Army for special missions. Similar versions for the Navy had all wheel drive.

1/2-Ton 4x4

The American Motors CJ-7 Jeep was purchased by all branches of the military in limited numbers, continuing a tradition that dated to World War II. This 1983 version belonged to the Air Force's 7219 Red Horse construction battalion at Spangdahlem AFB, Germany. Fitted with a 2.5-liter four-cylinder gasoline engine and four-speed synchromesh transmission, this one also featured the factory hardtop and metal doors.

When Mercedes-Benz introduced its G Type vehicle in 1981, there was some speculation it might be brought to the United States. Unfortunately, most Americans who have driven one have done so while assigned to the Army in Germany. These 246 GD models were bought in 1986 and served the Military Police in Grafenwohr. They used a 72-horsepower, 2.4-liter four-cylinder diesel engine and a four-speed synchromesh transmission.

The advent of the redesigned Jeep Cherokee in 1984 gave the government an opportunity to buy a light, practical all-wheel-drive utility vehicle at reasonable cost. They are a common sight on military bases around the world, essentially becoming the civilian replacement for the M151. AMC's inline 2.4 liter six-cylinder engine and a four-speed transmission in a two-door body were the initial purchase, but in subsequent years, many have had four doors and an automatic transmission. *BK*

3/4-TON 4x4

Around 1986, American Motors announced a model YJ-L long wheelbase military version of their Wrangler pickup. It was an eight-person troop carrier that could be adapted to many military uses. By 1991, when this photo was taken, it was fitted with a Cummins B3.9 105-horsepower engine (a 120-horsepower version was optional), and had a Chrysler A727 three-speed automatic transmission and New Process Model 231 two-speed transfer case. With a range of over 400 miles and the legendary durability of the Jeep product, it has been sold to several foreign governments. *MFG*

The competition to provide vehicles for special operations has been formidable in the past few years. The events in the Persian Gulf proved the usefulness of these little rigs in modern times, and in 1994, General Motors built a few of these Light Tactical Trucks for evaluation by military agencies. Using their K30903 chassis with open cab and folding windshield as the base, a cargo body with canvas tarp was provided, along with GM's 5.7-liter 180-horsepower V8 engine and four-speed automatic with overdrive. *MFG*

2 1/2-Ton 4x4

In 1984, the Army bought several hundred of these Mercedes-Benz Unimog U 1300 L models. Capable of operation in the worst conditions, they utilized an OM352 six-cylinder diesel engine and a split gearbox with a planetary gearset behind the main transmission, giving eight fully synchronized speeds forward and reverse. M-B's portal axles were fitted, offering more than 17 inches of ground clearance, and they used 12.5R20 cross-country tires.

Similar to the Army's 4x2 Ford trucks built for special missions, this was a 4x4 version built for the Navy a few years earlier. Based on Ford's F-700, this one was modified in 1992 by Fontaine Equipment of Louisville, Kentucky, for work along the coastlines. The dual rear tires assisted when negotiating sandy beaches, and the 5,000-pound front winch was provided for self-recovery. Extra fuel tanks more than doubled the travel range. *FE*

By 1995, the Navy had modified its special mission Ford vehicles to carry a Reading utility body, and had upgraded the chassis to the F-800 series. The trucks were used by the SEALs, and carried Ford's model 250 diesel engine, an Allison MD350 five-speed automatic transmission, 11R22.5 Goodyear tires, 12,000-pound Marmon-Herrington front and 21,000-pound Rockwell rear axles, along with a 5,000-pound front recovery winch. A 1997 edition even had polished aluminum wheels. *GS*

In 1981, the Air Force purchased a small fleet of these Revcon Model T30 front wheel drive vans to carry their personnel records management system for the tactical environment, known as PERSCO. It was a computerized system, and the prime contractor was General Electric. The front drive was a modified Oldsmobile Toronado with a gasoline V-8 engine and turbo Hydramatic. Weighing in at 15,500 pounds, they were air transportable to the combat zone. The Army owns some similar Revcons for calibration of special weapons.

Clegg Industries of Victoria, Texas, built this unusual van in the summer of 1990 for the Army's 82nd Airborne Division at Fort Bragg, North Carolina. It uses an Oldsmobile Toronado drive train, with V-8 engine and automatic transmission,

with drive only on the front axle. It is a telemetry van, capable of receiving and analyzing electronic transmissions during operations involving air drop of personnel and equipment.

10-Ton 6x4

The Army tries to include as much realism as possible in its training environments, and in an effort to replicate the communications equipment used by the enemy, someone decided that an American Autocar somehow resembled an East European or Russian heavy truck. Known as the XMG1S, at least the electronic element does have the capability of simulating the data link signals and air battle management requirements of the enemy. *ARMY*

15- to 20-Ton 6x4

Air Force 5,000-gallon aircraft refuellers are designated as A/S 32 R9, and this R9 was based on a 1981 Mack DM492S chassis. It carried an aluminum tank with pump equipment by Kovatch, and was powered by a 210-horse-power Caterpillar Model 3208, coupled to an Allison MT643 four-speed automatic transmission. A Kovatch transfer case drove the Hale 600-gallons-per-minute centrifugal pump. Note that the muffler was mounted under the front bumper to reduce the possibility of igniting the fuel being dispensed. *AF*

Around 1984, the Army Engineers ordered some of these White Road Boss 2 long wheelbase chassis to carry a fully enclosed topographic (map making) support system in a detachable 20-foot container, which included its own electrical generator. The White had a Cummins NTC400 engine, Allison five-speed automatic transmission, and Eaton DT440P tandem drive axles. This particular one belonged to the Mississippi National Guard and was working at Fort Belvoir, Virginia.

When Oshkosh got the contract to build 6,000-gallon R-11 refuellers for the Air Force in 1987, they elected to design a totally new front sheet metal section, making the truck very distinctive in appearance. Almost 1,600 of them were built, all using a 250-horsepower diesel engine with five-speed automatic transmission. The non-driven front axle had a 16,000-pound capacity, and the tandem rear was rated at 52,000 pounds. The roll-up control panel door shows the Kovatch pumping equipment.

Since the warheads are not generally kept on the underground Minuteman II missiles, they must be ready on short notice to be moved to the site. These 1991 Kenworth tractors are the Payload Transporters, and the auxiliary power unit mounted just behind the cab will provide the electrical power to operate the handling equipment in the semi-trailer.

The AM General M915 tractors have provided excellent service since 1977, with the M915A1 upgraded in 1981 to replace the original 16-speed semiautomatic transmission with a fully automatic five-speed Allison. In 1990, Freightliner got the new contract, and the M915A2 is the result. The front end is more aerodynamic and tilts for access, it has an aluminum cab, and anti-lock brakes. The new engine is a Detroit Diesel Series 60 with 400-horsepower from 12.7 liters displacement, while a four-speed Allison HT-740 transmission is standard. *BK*

The George E. Failing Company of Enid, Oklahoma, built this water well drill rig in 1990. A total of 18 were purchased in support of Desert Storm, along with 13 support vehicles that carried a generator, water, pipe, and other supplies for the drill rig. The chassis was an International F1954 with a DTI-466C 210-horsepower diesel engine, five-speed transmission and two-speed transfer case, and there was an on-board welder, air compressor and generator. This drill was working in the sands of Saudi Arabia when photographed by *Stars & Stripes* staffer Ken George. *SS*

The Air Force ordered this 1995 L-9000 series Ford for use at Dover AFB, Delaware. Featuring a Century 45-ton wrecker body, the long wheelbase truck had a Detroit Diesel 11 liter series 60 engine and an Allison HT-750 five-speed transmission. The front axle was a 12,000-pound Rockwell, and the Hendrickson tandem at the rear was rated at 56,000 pounds. *ME*

Although Oshkosh built nearly 1,600 of the Air Force's A/S 32 R-11 refuellers in the 1980s, the latest contract went to the Volvo Corporation, and the 1997 R-11 has the appearance of the late White GMC conventional truck. Kovatch Mobile Equipment is still the provider for the pump and 6,000-gallon tank assembly. Recently delivered to Pope AFB at Fayetteville, North Carolina, the new Volvo can expect to see more than 10 years of service.

5-Ton 6x6

Appearing to be every inch a strictly commercial International Model F-1954, this 1987 6x6 actually shows some modifications for air transport: a sling lift/tie down front bumper is obvious, as is the flattened roof and removable exhaust pipe. This is one of several dozen modified by Kaffenbarger for the Air Force. *KF*

10-Ton 6x6

Although Libya has had strained relations with the United States for years, there have been occasional sales of motor vehicles to them. This FWD RB series 10 tonner was shipped to the Libyan Army in about 1985, and was configured as a tractor with fifth wheel. The outside tires of the tandem set and the spare are banded on the rear for shipment. Technical details are not known, but the RB normally used a Cummins NTC 300-horsepower engine and a 10-speed manual transmission. *MFG*

10-Ton 6x6

The AM General M920A1 chassis was used as the platform for this Century Model 1045-M wrecker, which had a 45-ton capacity. It was sold to the Navy c. 1987, and incorporated two amidships winches with dual cables and hooks, along with hydraulic ground anchors at the rear for stability in heavy lifting. The powertrain would have been the normal M920A1: a Detroit Diesel Series 60 400-horsepower engine and an Allison five-speed automatic transmission. *EC*

This clean Mercedes-Benz Type 2628 was delivered to the Army in Grafenwohr in February 1988, equipped as a tractor for semitrailer. As comfortable as a luxury car, the 2628 had an M-B diesel V-8 engine that developed 280 horsepower, a six-speed synchronized transmission with two-speed transfer, 12R22.5 tires, and a road speed of 50 miles per hour.

The Air Force's construction battalion, Red Horse, has a fleet of these Oshkosh Model F2546 SPCL 6x6 trucks with McNeilus MTM cement mixers aboard. The 8-cubic-yard mixer is driven from a PTO at the front of the truck engine, which is a Cummins Model LTA 10-220, with 220 horsepower. Delivered in the late 1980s, they used a Fuller nine-speed transmission, Oshkosh two-speed transfer, with Oshkosh front axle and Rockwell tandems at the rear.

AM General had the original contract for the M915/916 series trucks, which were based on Crane Carrier Corporation's cab and chassis. By 1983, the series included this M918 asphalt distributor with tank, heating, and spreading equipment by Etnyre. The truck chassis used a Cummins NTC400 diesel engine, with a Caterpillar 16-speed semi-automatic transmission and an Oshkosh single-speed transfer. *ET*

The AM General M916 became a Freightliner M916A1 when the contract was re-awarded in 1989, and the new truck features an Allison four-speed automatic transmission with a two-speed transfer case, with a Detroit Diesel Series 60 engine with 400 horse-power from 12.7 cubic liters. This truck returned to Fort Knox from the Persian Gulf, and still wears the light sand paint job.

The 6x6 M916A1 chassis is used under this dump truck, which carries a 14-cubic-yard body. It has the same basic character istics as the tractor version: aerodynam-ic tilting hood and fenders, an aluminum cab, all wheel drive with tandem lockup, and an anti-lock brake system. The transmission is a four-speed Allison HT-740 with torque converter, and the transfer is a two-speed Oshkosh. *MFG*

A wrecker version of the M916A1 by Freightliner has also been offered to the military, but neither type has yet been accepted for service. The specifications of the wrecker are similar to those of the dump, but there is a 20,000-pound self-recovery winch up front, a 45,000-pound main winch, and a 30,000-pound crane with an extended length of 18 feet. A 916A1 with a 7.5-cubic-yard concrete mixer is also available. *MFG*

25-TO 50-TON 6X6

A giant by anybody's standards is this Oshkosh Model K-2358 (6x6), which served as a transporter for the old MX intercontinental ballistic missile (ICBM). Seven were built in 1981, using a Cummins KTA-600 diesel, which developed 600 horsepower and worked with an Allison CLBT-6061 automatic transmission. A 20,000-pound Oshkosh front axle and 53,000-pound Rockwell rear tandem were used, with a GCWR about 160,000 pounds. The tractor alone weighed 31,560 pounds. *MFG*

The Army's M911 Oshkosh HET tank transporter tractor did have some competition in the development phase. This Autocar 6x6 is configured just as the M911 was, with three driving axles and a non-driven central pusher axle. Built around 1980, it had essentially the same drive train as the M911: A Detroit Diesel 8V-92T engine, Allison five-speed transmission with lockup, a Fuller two-speed auxiliary, and Eaton axles, along with two Braden 45,000-pound winches behind the cab.

Although this FWD Model RB662158 was never adopted by any U.S. agencies, it was offered as a candidate for the Heavy Equipment Transporter (HET) in 1980. A Cummins NTC 350 turbocharged diesel with 350 horsepower was teamed with a Fuller 10-speed manual transmission and an FWD two-speed transfer. An 19,220-pound FWD front axle was used, with 58,000-pound Rockwell tandem at the rear. An amidships 90,000-pound winch was also included. *MFG*

The Hendrickson Manufacturing Company also built a contender for the HET program, using a Cummins NTC-475 twin turbocharged six-cylinder Diesel and a Fuller RTO 10-speed transmission with Fabco two-speed transfer. An 80-ton capacity DP dual drum hydraulic winch was mounted behind the cab. The rig is shown here with a M60A1 medium tank aboard the trailer while being evaluated by the Army. The eventual winner of the contract was Oshkosh's M911. *MFG*

25-Ton 8x4

The 8x4 prime mover, which GMC and Goodyear Aerospace built around 1965 for the Minuteman missile, had to be upgraded as the weight of the missile and its trailer was increased. This led to the installation of a tag axle behind the rear driving tandem set in about 1972, so the truck acquired a 10x4 drive configuration. The original engine was still used, a 275-horsepower GMC V-12 gasoline model, with 275 horsepower from 702 ci. *DP*

Several fascinating vehicles were acquired from East Germany for use in Desert Storm. The Czech Tatra trucks proved to be quite useful, and were quickly adopted by the Americans. This is a Model 813 Kolos, which used Tatra's 270-horsepower 1,076-ci (17,640 cc) air-cooled V-12 engine, a five-speed transmission, two-speed auxiliary, and tandem steering axles up front. All Tatras feature swinging half-axles with torsion bar suspension. *AD*

A four-door crew cab Tatra 815 was included among the vehicles taken to Desert Storm by the Americans, and this one is towing a low boy trailer with a Bradley Fighting Vehicle aboard. The 815 used a 19,000-cc V-12 engine with five-speed transmission and two-speed auxiliary. The American troops were able to employ most of the Tatras as prime movers, and especially appreciated the roomy six-man cab, which could be tilted for maintenance. A total of 200 Tatras were taken to Saudi Arabia, and some were returned to Germany to be destroyed in the mutual military equipment reduction program. *AD*

This strange device carries an 8 x 8 x 20-foot container, offering hydrostatic drive and variable ground clearance. Built by Standard Manufacturing Co. of Dallas, Texas, it is known as their Rough Terrain Container Straddle Truck. The engine is a Detroit Diesel 8V92T, which develops 736 horsepower and powers a hydraulic pump. All wheels and the trailing arm suspension are controlled by hydraulics. It employs pivot steer, and the 16.00R25XS Michelin tires have a central inflation system. *MF*

30-Ton 10x6

As the Air Force's ICBM known as the Minuteman got bigger, so did the equipment used to carry and emplace them. The current "TE" unit (transporter-erector) is a 1992 Peterbilt, modified by the Loral Corporation. The Peterbilt tractor costs $1 million each (the trailer without a missile costs another $1.5 million each), and features a 450-horsepower Cummins engine, Allison HT eight-speed transmission, Rockwell axles, and 11x22.5 tires. The GCWR is 76,650 pounds.

This in-shop shot shows the dramatic length of the Minuteman II Peterbilt tractor. The entire unit is designated by the Air Force as their A/S 32 A-40, and the tractor has a 209-inch wheelbase measured to the center rear axle. The tires are 11x22.5, and there are 16 of them. An Onan auxiliary power unit mounted behind the tilt cab powers the hydraulics for trailer erection, landing gear, and powers the truck's electrical system when the main engine is shut down. *CC*

CHAPTER FOUR

EMERGENCY VEHICLES

The nature of emergency vehicles has varied dramatically over the past 20 years due to state-of-the-art technology changes. The design of a particular vehicle also tends to vary based on the specific need at the location where the equipment is being used.

The most common vehicles, of course, are the fire engines, or pumpers, but there are now several varieties of even this basic unit. Smaller fires often do not require a full size pumper, so "first out" or mini-pumpers are found at many military fire stations, and there are even very small models for indoor industrial use. All of these smaller trucks also require fewer operators while on the scene.

Brush trucks were once built behind the fire house using older vehicles as a starting point. But fighting fires over rough terrain can be a real challenge, and communities with large grassland or wooded areas now tend to have custom-built brush fire trucks available to ensure reliability and the presence of current technology.

All of these pumper types will generally carry a basic supply of water, foam, chemicals and hose, along with protective gear for the crew. Larger, more traditional pumpers will also carry ground ladders and other firefighting tools. The nature of many military installations will require that all wheel drive be available on at least one pumper, but this feature provides a safer truck on wet or slick roads as well as offering better cross-country ability.

The most useful and interesting type of emergency vehicle found in the military environment are the crash and rescue trucks. Many military installations have an airfield nearby, and when aircraft are present, the need for these specialized trucks increases accordingly. For the most part, the American military has simply ordered emergency vehicles, including crash trucks "off the shelf." After all, there are numerous commercial airports that have the same essential needs as a military airport. Even the need for all wheel drive is not limited to military airports.

The U.S. military does tend to buy its fire apparatus in quantity, just as it does other forms of transportation. It not only reduces cost, but the standardization also provides some interchangeability of components and makes it easier for personnel to move between assignments.

Of course, there are some highly specialized firefighters found in the military. The Navy uses very low silhouette fire trucks on its aircraft carriers, and there have been armored and tracked versions for use in hazardous environments. Tall buildings do not abound on military installations, but many of them do have a multi-story hospital, making aerial ladder trucks and telesquirt units a necessity.

Although fire apparatus make up the large majority of the emergency vehicles found in the military environment, there are also the necessary ambulances and emergency rescue vehicles, along with emergency command post and hazardous materials response units.

4x2

One of the smallest crash trucks is this A/S 32P-16A (Air Force) or TAU-3 (Navy), which was built by AOF-FILCO. Weighing a hefty 12,000 pounds gross, it carries 375 gallons of pre-mixed AFFF and 400 pounds of Halon 1211, and it can pump AFFF from the ship's system into its own tanks. Wedged into the frame is a Detroit Diesel 4-53N with hydrostatic drive to the wheels. It is only 41 inches high so it can easily move under parked aircraft. This particular TAU-3 serves on the U.S.S. *Saratoga*. *NAEC*

The U.S. Navy bought a small fleet of these Pierce Dash pumpers in 1986. They used a Cummins L10-300 six-cylinder diesel engine and an Allison HT-740 automatic four-speed transmission. A Waterous single stage 1,000-gallons-per-minute pump was mounted, and they carried 750 gallons of water and 100 gallons of AFFF. It also had a front-mount 5-inch intake, along with the usual rear intakes. *TS*

Cherry Point Marine Corps Air Station in North Carolina is the home of this 1987 Pierce with a 55-foot Tele-Squirt. Pre-installed piping allows the Squirt unit to reach high in the air to dispense the elements carried on board: 1,000 gallons of water, 750 gallons of AFFF, and 100 pounds of Purple K dry fire fighting agent. Five-inch intakes are mounted at the front and on the left side, and preconnected crosslay hose can be seen just above the pump panel. *JA*

A much-needed rear mount aerial was delivered to the Americans at Vilseck, Germany, in 1988. It is an IVECO (Magirus-Deutz) Type 140-25 chassis, with Type DLK 23-12 Vario 90-foot rear mount aerial ladder with waterway and work bucket by Magirus as well. The ladder can depress to -15 degrees or elevate to +75 degrees and rotate 360 degrees. A Deutz air-cooled V-8 with 256 horsepower is used, with a six-speed transmission with PTO to drive the hydraulic ladder mechanism and the centrifugal pump.

A/S 32 P-22 is the Air Force designation for this Kovatch Mobile Equipment pumper, which can be found on nearly every continent. Utilizing an extended cab, which provides safety for the accompanying firefighters, it also has a top-mount control panel that allows the operator to see in all directions. Designed as a structural or brush truck, it has a Darley 1,000-gallons-per-minute pump and carries 600 gallons of water and 55 gallons of foam concentrate. A Detroit Diesel 6V-92TA engine and Allison four-speed transmission were fitted.

This rescue truck is a custom rig, built by Dover Technologies of Appleton, Wisconsin, on a 1996 Pierce chassis. It is assigned to Pope AFB near Fayetteville, North Carolina, and serves both the airfield and the base housing areas. The tilt cab has four doors, enabling the crew to ride out of the weather, and has an elevated roof for better light and visibility. Roll-up doors secure the rescue gear, while a large rear door gives easy access from behind.

This unusual crash truck is owned by the Army and is in use at Fort Eustis, Virginia. It is a 1983 Fire Tec that is stationed at the airfield, with 1,350 pounds of Purple K dry powder, and 250 gallons of 6% AFFF or Light Water. The spheres in the bed contain the Purple K, which is manufactured by Ansul. As a crash truck, the deck gun would have been the primary discharge monitor, as it could be used without the operators leaving the cab. JA

Cadillac Gage's Peacekeeper armored car was based on a Dodge 1-ton 4x4 truck chassis, with the armor plate body welded up and bolted to the truck frame. Generally used as a light security or riot control car, a few were built as armored ambulances. As with most field ambulances, this one did not feature patient support or trauma equipment, but was simply a patient transport vehicle to remove the injured out of the line of fire. MFG

In 1985, the Air Force began purchasing this Oshkosh crash truck known as their A/S 32 P-19A. They can now be found all around the globe and carry an 850-gallons-per-minute Hale pump and 1,000 gallons of water. There is a 130-gallon tank of AFFF, and a 250-gallons-per-minute discharge turret in the bumper and a 500-gallons-per-minute turret on the roof. It also carries 500 pounds of Halon 1211. A Cummins NTC400 diesel engine and Allison HT-750DRT five-speed automatic transmission are fitted, and it has the ability to pump water or chemicals while still moving.

This 1986 Mercedes-Benz Type 1222AF has been fitted with a Type 16/25 pumper apparatus body by Ziegler. A crew cab allows the firefighters to travel in safety, while all side compartments are protected by roll-up doors, and ground ladders are carried on the top. It carried 2,500 liters of water, and 200 liters of foam, and had a Ziegler 800-gallons-per-minute centrifugal pump, which was driven by the V-6 Mercedes-Benz 168-horsepower diesel. The rig is assigned to the Army's 26th Support Group in Heidelberg, Germany.

In 1988, Amertek, of Woodstock, Ontario, began delivery to the Army of a new fire truck that would handle aircraft crashes, fire and rescue operations, and which could fight ground and structural fires as well. It was known as a multipurpose truck, Model 2500L. It featured a 1,000-gallons-per-minute Godiva single stage centrifugal pump, and carried 660 gallons of water and 72 gallons of foam. Three hose reels are on top of the aluminum body, with 50 feet of 1-inch hose each. Note the top-mounted control panel. A Detroit Diesel 6V92TA gave 350 horsepower, and an Allison five-speed automatic had a Chelsea PTO to drive the pump. The Amertek is now found at nearly every Army post.

This formidable creature is a brush truck, and the builders were quite serious about breaking through whatever vegetation stood in the way. Based on a 1988 Dodge 350 Power Ram cab and chassis, it sports a front-mounted self-recovery winch, an auxiliary engine for the 250-gallons-per-minute pump, and a handy array of cabinets to protect the loose equipment. It carried 150 gallons of water and had space for firefighters at the rear. All wheel drive and tandem rear wheels assisted in travel over rough terrain at Fort Dix, New Jersey.

The four-wheel drive edition of the Air Force's P-22 is this A/S 32 P-24, which is also built by Kovatch Mobile Equipment. Issued to Bitburg AFB, Germany, in 1990, it also uses Detroit Diesel's 6V-92TA engine but with a five-speed Allison automatic transmission and a two-speed transfer case. The 4x4 feature allows it to move off of improved roads, and a 20,000-pound self-recovery winch is provided at the front. A Darley 1,000-gallons-per-minute pump can draw from the 600 gallons of water aboard and 55 gallons of foam. A front intake is mounted to the right of the winch, and there are intakes on both sides and at the rear.

Kovatch was the builder of this compact and useful A/S 32 P-20, which was delivered to Bitburg in July 1991. Based on a Ford F-350 4x4 chassis, it carried Purple K and Halon 1211 for combating aircraft or structural fires. A separate hose reel serviced each of the agents, while halogen lights could be elevated to better illuminate the fireground.

This 1990 Wheeled Coach ambulance was totally equipped to respond with trained Emergency Medical Technicians, and offered everything but an operating room while en route to a fixed facility. It could carry three patients and still have room for the attending technicians. Doors at the right side and at the rear gave excellent access. It was based on a Ford F-350 4x4, with a 7.3-liter diesel engine and four-speed automatic overdrive transmission with two-speed transfer.

Although it looks like a 6x6, this Faun LT 22.30/45V with Ziegler apparatus only drives on the first and third axles. Powered by a rear-mounted Deutz V-8 air-cooled diesel of 320 horsepower, it has a four-speed ZF automatic transmission, and a 60-miles-per-hour top speed. Built in 1984, it carried 923 gallons of water, 74 gallons of foam concentrate, and 1,650 pounds of dry chemical. A 740-gallon-per-minute Ziegler centrifugal pump was used, driven from the main PTO, and there were 240 feet of 2 1/2-inch hose on four electric reels, plus the roof monitor. *BK*

6x4

Fort Knox, Kentucky, has a tall apartment complex and a nine-story hospital that require protection by this 1993 Pierce 105-foot rear-mount aerial ladder with pre-piped waterway to the tip. The aerial ladder is a four-section unit that is actuated by hydraulics, with a manual backup that can rotate 360 degrees. The rear mounted turntable gives excellent access for firefighters from either side, while four stabilizing jacks can be adjusted for uneven terrain.

6x6

The Kentucky Air National Guard owns this 1987 A/S 32 P-18 built by Kovatch. It carries 2,000 gallons of AFFF, 500 gallons of water, and has a 1,000-gallons-per-minute centrifugal pump. Essentially a crash truck, the 38,000-pound International Paystar is driven by a Detroit Diesel 6V92TA engine with 350 horsepower from 552 cubic inches and has an Allison HT750DRD five-speed transmission and two-speed Spicer transfer case. The tires are 18Rx22.5 singles all around.

Oshkosh builds their Model DA-1500 Aircraft Rescue and Firefighting Vehicle on a custom basis for protection in rough terrain away from the runway. A descendent of the articulated Lockheed Dragon Wagon of the 1970s, Oshkosh has developed it into a fast and efficient crash truck. It can reach 50 miles per hour in 40 seconds, powered by a Detroit Diesel 8V-92T engine with 540 horsepower, and that is coupled to a five-speed Allison CLT-755 automatic transmission with a two-speed transfer case. The 1,200-gallons-per-minute two-stage centrifugal pump has its own engine, a 300-horsepower Detroit Diesel 6V-53TA. It carries 1,500 gallons of water and 265 gallons of foam, and it has a roof monitor, along with ground sweep nozzles to protect the truck itself. *MFG*

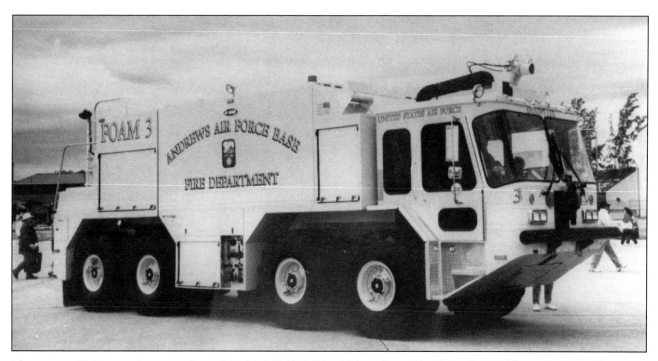

The current Air Force primary crash truck is the A/S 32 P-23, which replaces the 65-ton P-15 of the early 1980s. The P-23 is much lighter, at only 38 tons loaded, and is so agile in rough terrain it could be a Jeep. This agility is due to its independent suspension on all eight wheels, allowing 15 inches of vertical wheel travel, and to a central tire inflation system. It is powered by a 575-horsepower Detroit Diesel engine and has a Twin Disc transmission. Air disc brakes are used all around, along with differential locks on the axles and inter-axles. It carries 3,300 gallons of water, 500 gallons of foam concentrate, and 500 pounds of dry chemicals. The pump is an 1,800-gallons-per-minute centrifugal, located at the rear of the vehicle. For pump-and-roll there are roof and bumper turrets, and for structural fires there are four 2 1/2-inch discharge gates and one 1 1/2-inch preconnect. It is built by Emergency-1 and Oshkosh. *GS*

CHAPTER FIVE

TACTICAL TRUCKS

The story of the development of tactical wheeled vehicles in the United States in the past 15 years is rather phenomenal. Nearly every type we use has been recently replaced with new models.

It has not always been so easy to find a new truck in the inventory. Since the early 1950s, when the M series 2 1/2-ton, 5-ton, and 10-ton 6x6 trucks were introduced, those venerable machines have soldiered on, often with repairs and rebuilds too numerous to mention. The last new medium 6x6 was built around 1975. Many of them are still in service. The last new Jeep was built in 1985, and they have only recently been removed from service.

The feeling after World War II had been that the vehicles used in that war had been OK, but they had been based on civilian trucks modified for military use. That they had won the war was irrelevant. What the military really needed, the argument went, was trucks that were designed from the ground up for a military mission. So the new M series were designed as tough, practical, heavy vehicles that would last for several decades.

But they were also somewhat over-engineered. In designing them, we ignored the fact that most of our allies, including the technically proficient Dutch and Germans, were designing their postwar military tactical trucks using a clean sheet of paper, and were including some startling technical advances. Oversized single tires, cab-over-engine configurations, and diesel engines were major features of our allies' new truck designs.

By employing a single oversize tire on each axle end, the Europeans were saving dramatically on the unsprung weight for each axle or tandem set of axles, and saving in the long run on tire replacement costs as well. Unlike civilian trucks, military trucks in a peacetime environment rarely carry their maximum loads for prolonged periods, so those eight rear tires on an American 6x6 were usually just wearing out needlessly.

Then there was the cab configuration to consider. American military trucks have predominantly been of a conventional design, with the cab behind the engine. This of course, limits the driver's visibility close to the front of the truck, but does allow for a full opening hood for easier engine access. Our European and British counterparts opted for the cab-over-engine design. It saved space, which can be rather precious when loading a ship or an aircraft; gave the driver a much better view of the road; and if properly engineered, allowed much of the engine heat to flow out below the cab instead of being absorbed by the firewall and floorboards. Engine accessibility could be managed by having the cab tilt forward for maintenance.

Diesel engines had a bad reputation in the United States for many years, and they were not readily accepted into the American military vehicle fleet either. The military tried other means of getting better reliability and fuel mileage without resorting to using a pure diesel. Believing that the next war would be fought on the plains of Central Europe, and aware that diesel fuel would be more readily available there than gasoline, a multi-fuel engine was developed for American military trucks. This engine could supposedly run on almost anything from olive oil to high grade gasoline with

The 1/4-ton 4x4 utility truck has served the American economy well since 1942. It was an American invention, and it is replicated today all over the world for use by both civilians and military. Known generically as the "jeep," they were traditionally inexpensive to own and operate, and if properly driven, they nearly always got through. The last of the jeep types was the M151 series, and despite some tricky handling characteristics and more than a few fatalities over the years, it too, served the Army well. The tendency of the M151 to go belly-up when maneuvered injudiciously led the Army to belatedly develop a rollover protection system for them in 1988. The kit included roll bars with shoulder belts, side doors, and floor modifications, as shown here on an M151A2. But it was all rather pointless, as the new HMMWV was already in production, with none of the handling problems of the M151. Actually, the last M151s were built in 1988, when 1,000 of them were produced for Pakistan by AM General.

only a little tinkering with the fuel system. The concept worked to some extent, but unfortunately these engines did not run very well on any fuel, including the gasoline.

Add to the equation the fact that someone had decided that if we were to fight in Central Europe, there would be dozens of rivers to cross, and since the bridges would surely be destroyed, all of our tactical trucks must be able to wade through streams. So our tactical trucks were equipped at the factory with waterproofed ignition systems. Unfortunately, testing had not shown that condensation has a tendency to form inside these watertight devices, shorting everything out until each element was disassembled and dried out, a very labor-intensive and time-consuming process.

Finally, in the late 1980s, we had the diesel engine. It was installed in the late versions of the M800 series 5-ton 6x6s, and was in all of the M900 series 5 tonners, which are still in use. True, it was much improved from the 1950s, and was not as "smelly, noisy, and smoky" as before. Most of the 2 1/2-ton 6x6s never got a diesel. Amazingly, as the M900 series trucks (introduced around 1983) got into production, there were some versions that used super single tires instead of duals at the rear. Today, the only 5-ton M900s with duals are the wreckers. But with the M900 we still had an engine hood that gave the driver no view of the road for at least 25 feet.

When the specifications for the new Family of Military Tactical Vehicles (FMTV) went out for bid a

1 1/4-Ton 4x4

When the Army asked for bids in 1981 for a truck that would replace several of its existing and aging tactical vehicles, five firms responded: Adcor, AM General, American La France, Chrysler, and Teledyne Continental. This was the running prototype by American LaFrance, designated as their Modular Desert Vehicle (MDV) Mark 1. It used a Deutz five-cylinder air-cooled 100-horsepower diesel with a four-speed transmission and two-speed transfer. It had solid axles, with 6,000 and 7,500 pounds rating, front and rear respectively. With 10,000-pound GVW, it sat on a 110-inch wheelbase. The body was built by Pierce Manufacturing of Appleton, Wisconsin. *MFG*

The second version of American LaFrance's HMMWV candidate was this Multi Duty Vehicle (MDV), which the company rated at 2 1/4 tons capacity. Still using the Deutz engine and Warner T19A transmission, the GVW was up to 11,000 pounds, with 6,240 being the curb weight of the truck. The front axle was rated at 5,700 pounds, the rear at

7,500, both limited slip models with a 46:1 ratio. The tires were 12.5x16.5. A normal tailgate was fitted at the rear for access to the cargo bed while a 25-gallon fuel tank gave a range of nearly 400 miles. *JM*

When the engineer working on the American LaFrance HMMWV candidate moved from that firm to FWD, the project moved with him. FWD then fabricated this Modular Military Vehicle (MMV), which has many characteristics of the original MDV, including the Deutz engine. But a GM four-speed was fitted, and the MMV had a totally new body that was six inches lower at the base of the windshield than the MDV types had been. The MMV performed well in tests, but the expected production costs were $35,000 each v. $25,000 each for an AM General model, so the project was shelved. *RP*

few years ago, the competition had to have cab-over-engine (COE) design, diesel engines, and super single tires all around. It only took 45 years. They have some other nice features as well. Automatic transmissions are the norm, fully enclosed cabs are found on all of the new COE designs, and they even have central tire inflation systems, something that was pioneered on the amphibian DUKW in World War II, then used in Russian trucks of the 1960s.

Tactical trucks are not just restricted to the midrange cargo-carrying variety. The indomitable 1/4-ton 4x4 Jeep, which could be manhandled in bad terrain, was a tactical truck, and current wisdom says we no longer need them. The M151 series did have lots of problems, including 80 fatalities from 1977 to 1987 due to rollovers (nobody seems to have kept track of the tally from 1961 to 1977). It has been replaced by a 1 1/4-ton 4x4, which is as wide as a deuce-and-a-half and weighs twice as much as the Jeep did, but which is admittedly a remarkable vehicle. Known as the High Mobility Multipurpose Wheeled Vehicle (HMMWV or Hummer), the new truck has established a reputa-

tion for stability, strength, and reliability. And due to its formidable size, it can handle weapons systems that would have destroyed a 1/4-ton Jeep. Although the open Jeeps in their various forms were much fun and easy to maneuver, most of us would just as soon travel in the Jeep Cherokees, which the military has bought in amazing numbers. They have roll-up windows, heaters, and air conditioners.

Tactical trucks also exist at the huge end of the spectrum. The 8x8 and 10x10 Heavy Expanded Mobility Tactical Truck (HEMTT) models are amazing both in their size and in their cross-country ability. And the gigantic Heavy Equipment Transporter (HET) is not only immense, it is also a very handsome truck.

The most interesting aspect of American tactical truck development over the past 15 years is the fact that nearly every truck in the fleet, from the 1 1/4-ton HMMWV to the 25-ton HET, is a relatively new and modern design. Many thought it would never happen.

In the early 1970s, the Army wanted to remove the M274 Mule, M151 Jeep, and M561 Gama Goat from the inventory due primarily to age and safety considerations. A commercial alternative was wanted, which would be much less expensive than a tactical truck. Tests were run on pickups and sport utility vehicles by American Motors, Chevrolet, Dodge, Ford, and International. The original contract went to Dodge in about 1975 for the M880 pickup. The second contract for the Commercial Utility Cargo Vehicle (CUCV) went to Chevrolet in 1982, including this M1009 equipped with cold weather insulation gear. The holes in the radiator cover are for the slave connector (right side) and the blackout driving lamp (left). Power was by a 6.2-liter 135-horsepower V-8 diesel, and it used a GM three-speed automatic transmission, and a New Process two-speed transfer. *TAC*

The pickup version of the CUCV was designated as the M1008, seen here with a canvas top to protect the eight-foot-long cargo area. The rear bumper is a step type, but still incorporates the blackout lights, tie-down rings, and towing pintle. All of the CUCV models had matte paint that left no reflective surfaces except the glass. Many of the CUCVs were painted in four-color camouflage as seen here. *APG*

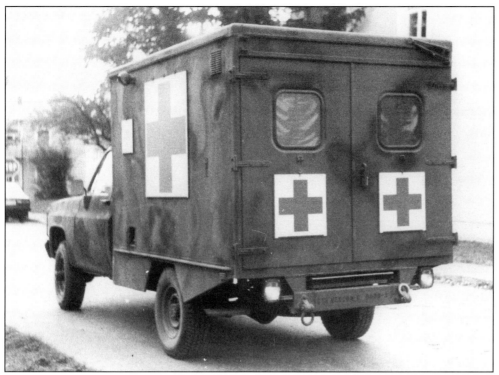

Chevrolet sent their 131.5-inch wheelbase M1031 cab and chassis to other manufacturers, who installed the ambulance body, creating this M1010. It was essentially a patient transfer vehicle, equipped to handle four litters, and had air conditioning and heating for the patient compartment. As with all CUCV models, it had an engine diagnostic system, slave start adapter, and multipurpose towing and tie-down eyes.

The CUCV carrier for shelter boxes was similar to a pickup, but had no tailgate, and had extra brackets to which the shelter could be secured. The basic truck without a shelter was designated as the M1028, and this particular one is carrying an S-250 Communications Shelter. There were numerous types of shelter boxes over the years, built by a large number of manufacturers, but most were similar to this one. *WES*

One of the less frequently seen CUCV variants was the M1031 cab and chassis fitted with a contact maintenance body. The contact truck never had an M-series designation of its own. The bodies were built by several manufacturers, and this one was by the Able Body Corporation, Model AGO-10, built in August 1989. Weighing 9,200 pounds gross, it carried an air compressor, chain saw, cut off saw, grinder, hammer drill, hydraulic pump, impact tools, vise, welder, and hundreds of other tools and fixtures.

The CUCV Chevrolets are now as much as 15 years old and are rapidly disappearing from the fleet, replaced primarily by the HMMWV. However, Chevrolet continues to market an updated version, known as their CUCV II. It uses a 5.7-liter 180-horsepower V-8 gasoline engine, with a GM four-speed automatic and overdrive. A two-speed transfer gets the power out to the axles, which are rated at 4,250 pounds front, 6,084 rear. The tires are LT245/75R16E, on 16x6.5 steel rims. Blackout lights are standard, as is the brushguard and a canvas top and bows. There is also a CUCV II ambulance. *MFG*

The Chrysler HMMWV candidate was eventually marketed by General Dynamics' Land Systems Division, and was offered to the Army in this configuration. As the competition for the HMMWV contract intensified, FWD dropped out, leaving General Dynamics, AM General, and Teledyne Continental. This was the General Dynamics prototype, as tested at Aberdeen Proving Ground during the winter of 1982. The Deutz 400-ci air-cooled V-8, 160-horsepower diesel was fitted, along with a Chrysler A727 three-speed automatic transmission, and New Process two-speed transfer case. *JS*

Teledyne Continental's entry in the HMMWV sweepstakes originally looked like this but was later modified to eliminate the bug-eyed look by use of rectangular sealed beams mounted lower in the body. This version was shown in the summer of 1980, and it featured an IHC 140-horsepower diesel engine, three-speed automatic transmission, two-speed transfer, and controlled-traction differentials. It could ford 30 inches of water (other makes needed a kit) with a 2,500-pound payload. The minimum height was 50 inches. *MFG*

When the Teledyne Continental candidate got to Aberdeen for tests in the fall of 1982, it had become considerably more sophisticated. Still using the International Harvester 6.9-liter, V-8 130-horsepower diesel, it also had a GM Model 475 THM three-speed Hydramatic transmission, Chrysler 208 two-speed transmission, and Dana axles with independent suspension all around. The variable rate suspension was by torsion bars, and it had four wheel disc brakes. It had a 130-inch wheelbase, and a turning radius of 25 feet. *JS*

This rear view of Teledyne Continental's standard ambulance indicates the arrangement for carrying four patients and the convenient access step, which folds out of the rear lower body. The ambulance box was made of ballistic fiberglass, designed to tolerate small arms fire as well as nuclear, biological or chemical environments. This ambulance configuration essentially is the same as that of the current HMMWV ambulance. *MFG*

This is AM General prototype for the HMMWV, which was first shown in the summer of 1981. Although it may have carried a fiberglass outer shell, the mechanicals were already taking their final form. A Deutz V-8 F8L610 air-cooled diesel with 160-horsepower was used, with a Chrysler A727 three-speed automatic transmission and NP 218 two-speed transfer case. The track was 71.5 inches, wheelbase 130 inches, and the turning radius was 24 feet. Independent coil spring suspension was used all around, and the tires were 36X12.5-16.5. By the fall of 1982, the use of Detroit Diesel's 6.2-liter V8 had been announced. *MFG*

The AM General HMMWV prototype looked like this by March 1983 when it was selected to be the new giant Jeep. The grille carried a bit of the World War II Jeep image, but otherwise it was a totally different animal. The initial contract was for nearly 55,000 of them, the largest contract the Army had ever awarded for a single type of vehicle, and a nice thing for the people of Mishawaka, Indiana, where they are still built. The initial publicity blurb said it would replace the M561 Gama Goat, M274 Mule, and some M151 Jeeps, and that it had a range of 300 miles, a top speed of 70 miles per hour, and could go from 0 to 30 miles per hour in eight seconds. *MFG*

Although similar to the previous prototype, this pre-production prototype of the AM General Hummer had a lower hood profile, cooling louvers on the hood, had lost its tie-down shackles, and has a larger windshield. This body was the weapons carrier configuration, with metal doors and a pop-up roof to enable it to carry one of several weapons systems being proposed. It had a full 16 inches of ground clearance, due primarily to the independent suspension system, and could go 65 miles per hour with a range of up to 350 miles thanks to a 25-gallon fuel tank. Note the lifting eyes protruding through the top of the hood. *MFG*

The testing of any vehicle at Aberdeen Proving Ground, Maryland, is intensive, and includes every operating condition one can imagine. Here an early production model of AM General's M1025 is emerging from a long trip through the water obstacle and is dumping some water from the interior. The external exhaust and elevated fresh air intake can be fitted as needed, and they were often spotted on HMMWVs in Desert Storm. The M1025 with a winch was designated as the M1026. *JS*

The pre-production prototype of the M996 mini-ambulance had a low profile, with only a two-litter capacity, as the roof did not elevate. The horizontal slat grille in this vehicle was designed to offer better protection for the radiator. Note that this truck has four windshield wipers, a feature later deemed unnecessary. The production mini-ambulance would eventually have a taller silhouette than this example. *MFG*

While at Aberdeen for its acceptance tests, this M1037 Shelter Carrier (without winch) posed for a portrait and displays the utilitarian nature of the HMMWV. Since the shelter slides along the entire 83-inch floor, the rear passenger doors are superfluous and have been blocked off. The GVW was 8,660 pounds, with 5,500 of that being the truck itself. Overall length was 188 inches, thanks to the towing pintle. The normal length was only 180 inches for all HMMWV models

except this one and the ambulances (203 inches). For the models with winches, the length was 186 inches, including the ambulances. *JS*

Although never considered for production, this useful little wrecker was assembled and demonstrated to the Army in 1988. It is based on an M1038 (with winch), and had handy tool compartments in the rear foot wells. The wrecker was operated hydraulically, with a winch mounted at the base of the boom to operate the lifting mechanism. The unit could effectively tow a similar size vehicle, i.e., one in the 8,000 to 10,000 GVW range. Unfortunately, the Army was not interested. *VPC*

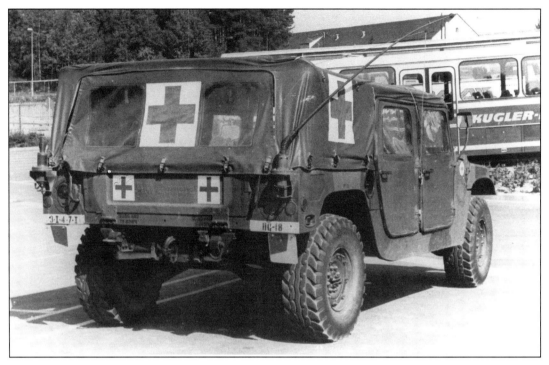

Before the first production HMMWV was built, AM General was bought by LTV Corporation, but it had no effect on the production schedule. However, the General Accounting Office had found that the prototype Hummers required too much maintenance. Expected to go 1,300 miles between even minor failures, they tended to go only 367 miles. But the problems were typical for a totally new truck, and by the time the vehicles went into production in the late summer of 1984, they were remarkably trouble-free. This was the M1035 Soft Top Ambulance, with an overall height of 72 inches.

Known as the M996 Mini-Ambulance, this one had an overall height of 87 inches and had a payload of 1,900 pounds. When the hinged rear doors were opened, the entry step could be lowered for easy entry, although the floor to ceiling height was only 49 inches. The patient compartment was 8 feet 6 inches long and could carry two litter patients or six ambulatory ones. The low profile was designed for use in forward combat areas, and for Low Altitude Parachute Extration (LAPES) from low-flying aircraft. *VPC*

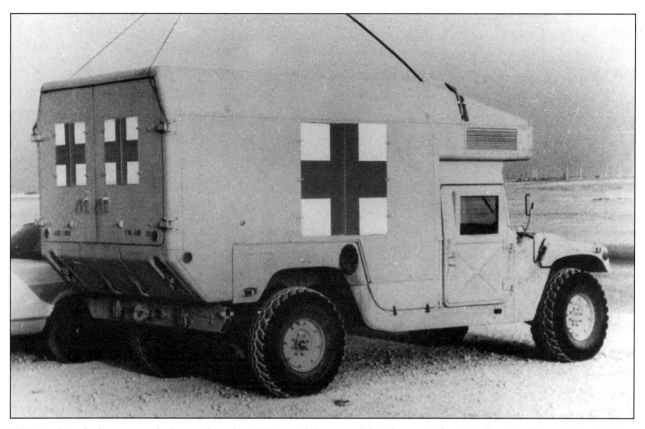

This Maxi-Ambulance was designated as the M997, and the overall height was 8 feet 5 inches. Both it and the Mini-Ambulance used a body structure that had fragmentation protection, but only the Maxi had an air conditioning and heating system for the patient compartment. The Maxi could handle four litters, or eight walking wounded. Both the Mini and the Maxi had heavy duty suspensions and 200-amp alternator to handle the extra loads. The M997 weighed in at 9,100 pounds gross, with 7,180 being the weight of the truck. *BK*

This prototype Desert Mobility Vehicle System (or DumVee) was designed for use with Special Operations and involves a HMMWV prime mover, which tows a specially adapted trailer. The M116A2 trailer is modified to carry a KL-250 D8 Kawasaki motorcycle, along with extra fuel, food, ammunition, water and other supplies to support an extended stay in the desert. This version involved an M998 troop carrier with winch, but a similar combination using an M1026 armament carrier was also tested. *GP*

The most basic HMMWV model was this M998 Cargo/Troop carrier, without winch. This was the troop seat version, and it could carry eight fully equipped troops, plus the two-man crew. Weighing in at 7,700 pounds GVW, the truck itself weighed 5,200 pounds. It was 85 inches wide, 180 inches long (as an M1038 with winch it would be 186 inches long), and the minimum height was 54 inches. Turning radius was 24 feet 4 inches, and the angles of approach and departure were 72 and 45 degrees, respectively.

With a winch, the M998 became an M1038, but otherwise they were identical. The winch was mounted at the front between the extended frame rails, and it was an electric unit with a 6,000-pound maximum capacity. Note that this unarmored HMMWV has seven louvers on the top of the hood. Of the original 55,000 HMMWVs built under the 1983 contract, 11,000 went to the Marine Corps, 1,100 to the Air Force and the remainder to the Army. By 1991, AM General had built another 40,000, for a total of 95,000 for the United States, and another 6,000 for foreign countries.

This is a worm's eye view of a HMMWV, and it helps explain why the truck has such a good reputation while going over rough terrain: nothing protrudes below the frame and main body to ever snag on a potentially damaging object. Suspension members elevate quickly out of the way, and differentials, oil sumps, fuel tank and muffler are all tucked neatly up into the crevices around the body. It also helps to explain why there is not much room up in the passenger compartment. *VPC*

This is what the driver sees in a HMMWV, minus the new vehicle stickers on the windshield. The engine switch is at the far left, with positions for glow plug warm-up, start, and stop, with the headlamp switch below it. The turn signal lever points upward to the left of the horn button. The usual fuel, oil pressure, coolant temperature, and voltmeter gauges

are clustered around the larger speedometer and odometer, and the switches to the right of that cluster are for the heater and defroster. Basically, an uncluttered design for a military vehicle, its instruments are over where the driver can easily see them. *VPC*

This M998 was configured as a four-door sedan, with a short pickup bed behind. The radios were mounted inside between the seats, and the antennae are tied down to prevent them from coming in contact with low-hanging power lines. As with all models, the M998 could climb a 60-percent grade, and travel on a 40-percent side slope. It had a cruising range of 300 miles on 25 gallons of fuel. The all-aluminum lower body was also shared with all other basic models.

This M1025 is the armament carrier, without winch. Known as the HUMMER 25, it has a remote electric drive turret (Red-T) on the roof, mounted in a 40-inch turret ring. It could slew 60 degrees per second through 360 degrees, and

was stabilized in elevation and azimuth when on the move. The gun is an M242 25mm Chain Gun, which could fire single shots or 200 rounds per minute. The gunner sat behind the driver watching a video screen that showed the target and gave pertinent data. The HMMWV had a ballistic windshield, doors, rear body panels, and engine air inlet grille. The total GVW was 8,600 pounds. The HUMMER 25 was never standardized. *AEB*

This M1026 Armament Carrier with winch has just been delivered to the Air Force at Ramstein AFB, and has no weapon system mounted. As with the Hummer 25, it has a ballistic windshield, doors, liftgate, rear quarter panels, and engine air inlet grille (with about 35 louvers), as well as having cowl and footwell armor. It will most likely eventually get a ring-mount M60 machine gun. The supplemental armor version (M1043 without winch, M1044 with winch) would have had smooth doors.

With the Tube-launched, Optically-sighted, Wire-guided (TOW) weapons system aboard, this M966 becomes a formidable anti-tank weapon. In fact, the number of M3 Bradley vehicles (Chapter 9) coming into the fleet was reduced to allow some of these HMMWV-based TOW missile carriers to take over the scout and reconnaissance role of the M3. The improved TOW 2 has a range of 3,750 meters, but the target must be in the line of sight of the operator. *ARMY*

There is considerable room inside the rear hatch area of a HMMWV, but it is quickly filled when the equipment supporting the TOW launcher is installed. Four missiles are seen here, along with the optical sight, a tripod for launching from outside the vehicle, the launch tube (attached to deck lid), and other smaller items. *JS*

Avenger fire units such as the one seen here were dispatched in 1996 to Bosnia, where they help protect elements of the 1st Armored Division. The Avenger is a surface-to-air missile, which is built by Boeing Aerospace. The pedestal turret contains eight Stinger missiles, and one .50 caliber machine gun, with the operator sitting under a ballistic shield in the center. The fire control equipment includes a forward-looking infrared sensor, laser range finder, heads-up optical sight, and a fire control computer. *MFG*

This prototype HMMWV was designed to carry eight Stinger missiles for the Avenger fire unit, but it was never put into production. The long side compartments contained two complete missile systems that could be employed in less than 10 seconds. Six more missiles were in the floor compartment behind the seats. Note the external mount of the extra jerry can. In 1993, LTV sold AM General to the Renco Group, about the time the HMMWV was upgraded to become the M998A1 series. The A1 models included an upgraded drive train and suspension, and greatly improved seats. *MFG*

Although it looks like an ambulance, this is actually a communications van for supporting electronic communications and general command and control of the battlefield environment. The system shown here is called the Intra-Vehicular Information System (IVIS), which allows tanks and artillery with compatible computers to communicate with each other, and allows reports and messages to be transmitted and received. There was access from the truck cab into the shelter, which also had heating and air conditioning.

The M998A1 series improvements were announced in the summer of 1993, and incorporated chassis components from the M1097 Hummer Heavy Variant, plus more comfortable front seats. From the HHV, the A1 got a new low range on the transfer case (2.72:1 v. the old 2.61:1), new axle ratios (2.73:1 v. the old 2.56:1) and a general upgrading of the drive train. It also got a metal hood grille, a solid state glow plug controller, and improved hand brake components, slave receptacle, and rifle mounts along with better rear axle half shafts. This M1097A1 is being loaded into a C-130 cargo aircraft. *MFG*

As with the CUCV, shelters come in a number of variations, including this one by Brunswick Defense. It is intended as a standardized, integrated command post, to handle whatever the mission requires. It had interior measurements of 81.5 inches (width), 99.5 inches (length) and 64.5 inches (height). It weighed 565 pounds empty but could handle 4,000 pounds. It was built of aluminum with a honeycomb inner wall and had electromagnetic shielding. *MFG*

A heavy version of AM General's product is this M1113 Expanded Capacity HMMWV (ECH). It has a payload of 5,150 pounds, and will accept such loads as a heavy shelter or an air defense weapons system. This one has the central tire inflation system, and all are fitted with the 6.5-liter turbocharged V-8 diesel with 190 horsepower, allowing acceleration to 50 miles per hour in 26 seconds despite its curb weight of more than 3 tons. The transmission is a four-speed automatic, and the axle ratios are 3.01:1 v. 2.73:1 in the standard HMMWV models. *MFG*

For environments where maximum protection is needed, this Armored Special Operations HMMWV is available from AM General. With a squareback design and opening rear cargo doors, it offers excellent accessibility and load space along with protection against small arms fire. This one is also fitted with a weapons station on the roof that would be used primarily during convoy duty. Based on an M1114 chassis, this one also has an elevated engine air intake and an extra capacity radiator to accommodate the turbocharged diesel engine. A similar XM1116 is going to the Air Force. *MFG*

The XM1097 was the Heavy Hummer Variant weapons carrier, and it carries the distinctive smooth doors with protruding glass pods, better armor protection for the engine's air grilles, and an armored weapons station on top. There was, of course, much more to the upgrade, with every angle protected by improved armor. With all optional armor mounted, it weighed over 8,000 pounds without a weapons system or passengers. The armor can defeat 7.62 or 5.56 ball ammunition at 15 feet fired at 90 degrees. This particular XM1097 also has the optional central tire inflation system. *MFG*

Another up-armored version was this A2-based XM1114, with modifications by O'Gara-Hess and Eisenhardt of Cincinnati, Ohio. It can defeat 7.62AP ammunition, 12-pound anti-tank mines, and 155 millimeter overhead airbursts. Fully loaded at 12,100 pounds, it has a 6.5-liter turbocharged diesel engine with 190 horsepower, and can out-accelerate other HMMWV models weighing a ton less. It has modified differentials, better disc brakes all around, improved engine cooling (note the extended fixed radiator grille), and upgraded suspension, wheels, and frame.

This is a lightweight variant which can be applied to the M998, 1025, 1037 or XM1097. Intended for quick desert operations, reconnaissance, and other special missions, it is a bare-bones HMMWV. As an M998, it would weigh only 7,700 pounds fully loaded. It can be selectively up-armored depending on the mission, including underbody crew protection. The central tire inflation system, lightweight weapons station, chassis skid plates, spare tire and jerry can carriers, extra radiator protection, brushguard, and a desert package for cleaner engine operation make it an ideal long distance patrol vehicle. *MFG*

This M1113 is yet another up-armored version, which was posed in 1995 in front of the O'Gara Hess & Eisenhardt plant where it was built for the Army. It offers 360-degree protection from 7.62 AP rounds from 100 meters, and the roof provides protection from overhead artillery bursts. The floor can handle the blast of a 12-pound anti-tank mine,

and the glass, including the roll-down door windows, is of transparent armor. The M1113 is based on the new M998A2 series, introduced in the fall of 1994. The improvements for the A2 included a 190-horsepower 6.5-liter V-8 naturally aspirated diesel, a four-speed automatic transmission, improved 9,000 pound winch, and creature comforts such as a better steering wheel, sunvisors, improved seats all around, better heating and ventilation, and west coast mirrors. *MFG*

This squareback design with elevated roof is found on Air Force bases and is used to carry electronics gear used for mobile ground-to-air communications. The upper body shell has a rear door, along with hinged access doors for the side compartments, and a high frequency antenna is mounted on the roof. The chassis is an M966A2 with basic armor and ballistic glass. Note that a wide brushguard is also fitted. Both brushguards and bumpers are routinely added by the using units to protect the fiberglass hood and fenders.

Equipped for long range patrol duty, this M1097A2 is known as the Special Forces Carrier by AM General, and is heavily modified to include front and side 7.62 weapons mounts and a cal.50 top-mount weapons station, with brackets for stowing extra gun barrels. It also has room for four seated passengers plus a standing gunner, infrared driving lights, central tire inflation, an improved 9,000-pound-capacity winch, and stowage cabinets for all of the supplies and equipment required for long stays away from base. It has no glass and, of course, no armor protection. *MFG*

From about 1977 to 1982, the J.I. Case Tractor Company marketed their model MB4/94 as an all-purpose utility vehicle that could mount a variety of implements. It was based on a Mercedes-Benz U-900 (406) Unimog chassis, and in 1980, a version was painted camouflage and offered to the American Army. It was a useful little rig, with a dozer

2-Ton 4x4

blade on the front, and a backhoe on the rear, with protection for the cab. It was also a relatively simple machine, with a 13,000-pound GVW, a Mercedes-Benz OM 352 six-cylinder diesel engine, with a cascade geared transmission with 14 forward and six reverse gears. *WES*

By mid-1982, the Unimog project belonged to Euclid, builders of giant earth-moving machines. It had been undergoing tests at Fort Lewis, Washington, since early 1981, and two types had evolved: the Small Emplacement Excavator (SEE) and the High Mobility Material Handling Equipment (HMMHE). The SEE had the blade and backhoe, while the HMMHE seen here had a forklift up front, and an 8,700-pound capacity crane at the rear with stabilizing jacks. Both machines were still fairly simple, but the GVW had been boosted to 16,000 pounds. A large variety of other interchangeable implements were proposed, including a snow blower, compactor, large winch, rotary broom, and trencher. *FB*

By 1985, Freightliner was the holder of the Unimog project, and along with the SEE and HMMHE, there was a Palletized Loading System (PLS) and a Tactical Explosives System (TEXS). However, the Army had only purchased the HMMHE and the SEE, seen here hard at work during Desert Storm. The 110-horsepower OM 352 was still used along with a 16-speed transmission (8 in reverse), with a PTO at each end driven from the transmission. Front and rear hydraulic systems operated the machinery. *AFCC*

In 1987, Freightliner announced the Unimog-based All Terrain Tow Vehicle (ATTV) tractor, which had a small cargo body to hold ballast, although the tailgate and sides could be removed. It had tow pintles front and rear, with the usual 16-speed (8 reverse) transmission, and it was evaluated by the Air Force for use as an aircraft tow tractor. As with the other variants, it had a top speed of 50 miles per hour, 12.5R20 12-ply tires, coil springs and disc brakes all around, and it could ford 30 inches of water. The angles of approach and departure for the ATTV were 33 and 60 degrees respectively. *MFG*

This was the HME, or High Mobility Entrencher, and it was designed initially as part of the TEXS system. It could cut a trench 8 inches wide and varying as deep as 7 feet. Hydrostatic drive was used to power the entrencher, and it offered a very slow ground speed while digging. The hydraulics on board also allowed for a concrete breaker, dewatering pump, and two-man earth auger. A front backfill blade was fitted, which was 84 inches wide and could be angled to 25 degrees right or left. *MFG*

The HMMHE was redesignated as the HMMH (High Mobility Material Handler), and is seen here with the forks down and ready to lift as much as 4,000 pounds as high as 8 feet 10 inches. Of course, they tilted forward and back and could even rotate plus or minus 15 degrees. The crane on the rear had a maximum lifting capacity of 6,000 pounds at an 8-foot reach, or 2,000 pounds when the boom was extended to 19 feet. The overall length was 17 feet 5 inches, the height was 8 feet 1 inch, and the width was 7 feet 9 inches. *MFG*

In 1991, AM General announced a new cab-over-engine tactical truck that was based on HMMWV components. Known as the COHHV (Cab Over Heavy Hummer Variant), it had many features of the XM1097 Heavy Hummer and was to be offered as the high bed model seen here and as a low bed type for carrying shelters. Due to the height of the cab, it could carry three occupants, and it had a 5,000 payload capacity for a GVW of 12,000 pounds. The cargo bed was 9 feet 9 inches long, and 6 feet 6 inches wide, with sides that dropped down for easier loading. The 6.2-liter 170-horsepower V-8 diesel of the HMMWV was used in the original truck, along with the three-speed automatic transmission and two-speed transfer. *MFG*

The low-bed version of the COHHV used the same chassis as the higher model, but was designed to accommodate shelter boxes. This facelifted version of the COHHV was still being marketed in 1994, and it had been upgraded along with the conventional HMMWV. The larger 6.5-liter 190-horsepower V-8 diesel was incorporated into the new version, along with the new four-speed transmission. A two-speed transfer housed the PTO. The optional hydraulic winch had an 8,000-pound capacity, or there was an electric winch offered rated at 9,250 pounds. The fording depth could be 60 inches with the correct options, and the operating range was listed as 400 miles based on the 48 gallons of fuel on board. *MFG*

3-Ton 4x4

It has been inevitable for years that the M series medium trucks would be replaced, and there have been enthusiastic proposals since the mid-1980s. Teledyne Continental demonstrated this prototype during the PROLOG '85 logistics exercise in May of that year. A tilt cab gave good access to the engine and cooling system, and the truck was only 20 feet long instead of the 23 feet of an M35 6x6. The top and windshield could be removed to lower the height to 81 inches. A Caterpillar model 3116 diesel with 250 horsepower was used, along with a seven-speed ZF automatic transmission and single-speed transfer case. In 1988, the Army contracted for 15 Teledyne trucks for further tests under the Family of Medium Tactical Vehicles (FMTV) program. *DAVA*

The new M900 series 5-ton 6x6 had been built by AM General from 1982 (M900 and M900A1), and by BMY from 1988 (M900A2), and it was natural to downsize this truck to a 4x4 for lighter duty. First shown in late 1991, it used a 240-horsepower Cummins 6CTA8.3 turbocharged diesel, a five-speed automatic transmission and two-speed transfer. It was still rather large, at 22 1/2 feet in length, 8 feet in width, and 9 feet 5 inches in height. The GVW was 23,080 pounds, with the payload being only 7,000 of that. The Marine Corps tested it, but it has primarily been built for the international market. *MFG*

Around 1988, Stewart & Stevenson built this contender for the FMTV program under a government contract. A long-time manufacturer of specialized heavy duty motor vehicles, they cooperated with Steyr AG of Austria and developed this truck. Fitted with Caterpillar's 3116 ATAAC engine with 225 horsepower from 6.6 turbocharged liters, an Allison MD-D7 seven-speed transmission and transfer, and Rockwell R-611 series axles front and rear, it sat on a 153-inch wheelbase, was 21 feet 5 inches long, and 9 feet 2 inches high. The angles of approach and departure were both 40 degrees, and it had 21 inches of ground clearance. *WES*

In October 1988, the Tactical Truck Corporation was also awarded a contract to build trucks for the FMTV program. TTC was a joint venture between General Motors and BMY, and this LMTV (light medium tactical vehicle) was the 3-ton contender. A Cummins 6CTA8.3 diesel engine was fitted with 225 horsepower from 8.27 liters displacement. A modular power pack joined the engine, seven-speed Allison transmission and integral transfer case. There was also a modular cooling system, and many of the mechanical and body components were interchangeable with their 6x6 version. *TAC*

The wheelbase of the TTC LMTV was 162 inches, the length was 21 feet, and the height was 8 feet 9 inches at the roof. With the roof, side windows and doors gone, and the windshield folded over, the height was considerably less. This is the fully drivable form it took when it was being prepared for air drop. The cab easily carried three troops. A central tire inflation system was used, and the axles were single speed Rockwell models. *MFG*

In October 1991, the contract for the Family of Medium Tactical Vehicles (FMTV) was awarded to Stewart & Stevenson, for both the 3-ton 4x4 and the 5-ton 6x6. There are four variants of the 4x4: the M1078 cargo truck, the M1079 van, the M1080 cab and chassis, and the M1081 air drop cargo. This M1078 weighs 16,206 empty, is 21 feet 1 inch long, 9 feet 4 inches high (8 feet 9 inches for air drop), and 8 feet wide.

The M1081 air drop version of the FMTV has a two-piece windshield, as well as hinges all around so the windshield and windows can be folded over to lower the profile. The roof is first lifted off and placed in the cargo bed. They all have full-time all wheel drive, a central tire inflation system, Allison seven-speed automatic transmission with integral transfer case, and Caterpillar's 6.6-liter turbocharged and aftercooled 225-horsepower diesel.

This is a pre-production prototype of the M1079, with van body. The height with the box is 11 feet 5 inches, the box has external electrical connections, and the interior dimensions are 12 feet long, 7 feet 6 inches wide, and 6 feet 6 inches high. This truck has the optional heater and air conditioner for the van, with the standard spare mount just below (behind the cab). A large engine air intake duct is also behind the cab on the driver's side.

In 1994, General Motors offered this GMC-based Commercial Enhanced-Mobility Medium-Duty Vehicle, or CEMMV. It is intended for the expanding international market and offers a relatively inexpensive 3-ton all-terrain cargo truck. With a GVW of 23,000 pounds, of which 6,600 is the payload and crew, it sits on a 195 inch wheelbase. A Caterpillar 3116 diesel is standard, with 250 gross horsepower, and it works with a four-speed Allison MT643D automatic and Rockwell two-speed transfer. It is also offered as a 6x6 with a 6-ton payload. *MFG*

4-TON 4x4

In about 1979, FWD International offered this Model RB441617 4x4 to the world market. It was derived from FWD's commercial Tractioneer series, modified for military use. It sat on a 168-inch wheelbase, relying on FWD's own axles, the front rated at 16,500 pounds, and the rear at 17,000. Cummin's Model PT240 diesel was fitted, with 230 horsepower and six cylinders. The transmission was a manual 10 speed, with a single speed transfer case. Michelin 14.00x20 sand tires were standard, as was the steel cargo body and sturdy brushguard, and a 10,000-pound PTO-driven winch. The GVW was 33,500 pounds. *MFG*

2 1/2-Ton 6x6

In 1978, Stewart & Stevenson was working with ESARCO of the UK to offer light, maneuverable military vehicles in the United States. This was an all-terrain vehicle, with steering on the front and rear axles, and coil spring suspension with shock absorbers at each wheel. A variety of engines was offered, including air or water cooled, diesel or gas. At only 12 feet 8 inches overall length and 6 feet 7 inches in width, it was a relatively small configuration. Similar in concept to the M274 Mule of an earlier era, most of the ESARCO was load space. *MFG*

Over the years, there have been many efforts to upgrade the existing fleet of 2 1/2-ton 6x6 trucks. In 1991, the Army asked for proposals for its Service Life Extension Program (SLEP), and in the summer of 1992, Cummins Military Systems Company agreed to provide eight remanufactured trucks for test. The vehicles were to employ Cummins' Model 6B5.9 diesel engine, new electrical systems, suspension systems, radial tires, and improvements in cab safety. A few were to have central tire inflation and automatic transmissions. This was one of the trucks submitted for evaluation.

SLEP became ESP (Extended Service Program) and the final contract went to AM General in the summer of 1993. Old deuce-and-a-half trucks are refurbished, and come out looking like this M35A3. A new Cummins 478-ci engine with 170 horsepower, a four-speed automatic transmission and two-speed transfer, new axles with super single radial tires, and a new cooling system are just starters. They also have split air/hydraulic brakes, better heat and air circulation in the cab, new power assisted steering, electric wipers and washer, and a central tire inflation system. The larger engine and cooling system were responsible for the headlamps moving to the fenders. Although early versions went to the National Guard, more than 1,000 are now going to Europe to the active army. *EK*

When the M939 series was first fielded in 1982, one of the nicest features was the tilting hood, which can be easily operated by one person, although it does not look that way in this view. This M923 got an automatic transmission, replacing the overworked five-speed manual in old M809 series. The manual two-speed transfer was also improved, with air actuation rather than the sprague clutch of the older type. The M800 had air-over-hydraulic brakes, while the new model had full air brakes. Tests showed that the new system wore out brake shoes at one fourth the rate of the older model. AM General was the prime contractor for the new trucks.

5-Ton 6x6

During 1985, the M939A1 series was released, and the major improvement was the use of super single tires all around, and some even offered a central tire inflation system, which AM General called their Enhanced Mobility System. The tires were noticeably larger (14.00R20 replacing 11.00x20). This particular winchless M923A1 had a rare hard top cab, which would have made it a bit quieter than the standard truck. The new series had reduced its noise level in the cab anyway by reconfiguring the air intake and exhaust systems. With a winch, it was designated M925A1.

This M927 without winch was carrying a removable container shelter on its long 215-inch wheelbase chassis. The immense bed easily handles a 20-foot box, in this case, part of a Patriot missile system. The engine used in the M939 series was Cummins' NHC250, which delivered 250 horsepower at 2100 rpm from 14 liters (855 cid) displacement. It was a six-cylinder naturally aspirated model. The long wheelbase truck with a winch was the M928.

Most 5-ton dump trucks belong to an Engineer unit, and this 22-foot, 9-inch-long M929 without winch was no exception. The snug-fitting tarpaulin helps to convert an open dump into a dry cargo truck, and of course, it would be removed for dump work. Weighing around 24,000 pounds empty, it could handle a 10,000-pound payload. As with all of the M939 models, the transmission was an Allison MT654CR, with five forward speeds, while the manual transfer case had two-speeds. With a winch, this was the M930.

The M931 tractor had the same mechanical features of the rest of the series, and when this M931A1 came along in the mid-1980s, it got a set of super single 14.00 R 20 tires all around. The overall length of the M931A1 was 22 feet, 6 inches and it was 9 feet 3 inches high at the top of the cab. The wheelbase was 13 feet 11 inches, and the track was 6 feet 6 inches. This tractor is pulling a M139A2 semi-trailer, which has a length of 28 feet. The M931 series with a winch was the M932. About 20,000 M939 series and about 4,000 M939A1 series trucks were built before the A2 series was introduced.

The Boyertown Auto Body Company built this 18-foot-long expansible van on AM General's M934 chassis. It had a wheelbase of 216 inches and an overall length of nearly 31 feet. The van expanded by manually cranking both sides out, for a maximum width of nearly 14 feet. While in the travel mode, the van is only 8 feet 2 inches wide. The M934 had normal rear opening doors, with a ground ladder attached to the left door for travel. The M935 expansible van had a hydraulic lift gate, with a pair of ground ladders attached for travel while en route. *MFG*

The workhorse of any tactical fleet is the wrecker, and this M936 is characteristic of a tactical wrecker. It has a 20,000-pound capacity winch in the frame extension ahead of the radiator and a 45,000-pound model behind the cab to operate the wrecker assembly. It has dual fuel tanks (139 gallons) to give a 400 mile range with a maximum towed load, 500 miles without. The hydraulic crane assembly can rotate 360 degrees and elevate to 45 degrees. With outriggers, the rear crane can support 20,000 pounds.

The M942, M943, M944 and M945 were all cab and chassis models, with the M943 and M945 versions being equipped with the 20,000-pound front winch. This is the winchless M944A1, carrying a Southwest Mobile Systems organizational repair Set 12. The huge 18-foot curved side panels elevated, giving access to the machine shop inside, and work platforms folded out, giving access to several hundred tools and maintenance items. Major components were a Hobart generator/welder, two air compressors, and a Hunter space heater.

Early in 1987, BMY of York, Pennsylvania, was building the new M939A2 series trucks in its Marysville, Ohio, assembly plant. While the upgrade for the 4,000 A1 variants had only involved the use of super single tires, the A2 models had a new Cummins 6CTA8.3 six-cylinder inline turbocharged and aftercooled diesel developing 240 horsepower from 8.3 liters. The transmission was an improved Allison MT654CR five-speed automatic, with a two-speed transfer. The lighter engine offered better fuel mileage, with a range just over 400 miles on 81 gallons of fuel. This M923A2 (925A2 with winch) also had central tire inflation.

This M927A2 (M928A2 with a winch) is the long wheelbase version of the new BMY-produced series. With a wheelbase of 215 inches measured at the center of the tandem bogie and an overall length of 380 inches (31 feet 7 inches), it has a rear overhang of about five feet. The normal drive train of Cummins 6CTA8.3 engine, Allison five-speed transmission, two-speed transfer, and single-speed double reduction axles applies to the M927A2. As with all A2 models, the super single 14.00R20 tires and central tire inflation system are used, evidenced by the triangular device on the front wheel.

A clean side shot of an M931A2 tractor without winch (this tractor with winch is an M932A2) shows the short length (265 inches, the shortest in the series) and swing-down feature for the spare tire mounted just behind the driver. Weighing 22,089 pounds, the M931A2 can tow a semi-trailer weighing 60,000 pounds, with 25,000 pounds of that on the fifth wheel. It is also obvious in this view that the large, square hood seriously restricts the driver's view of the road surface for about 25 feet. The wrecker version was the M936A2, and the 5-cubic-yard dump was the M929A2.

This large version of the M945 left BMY as a cab and chassis in 1987, and Southwest Mobile Systems Inc. added their Ribbon Bridge Transporter. The bridge element is elevated by an A-frame, which pivots at the rear, raising the hollow sections at the front, then moving them downward toward the water where they open out and become a floating bridge section. The entire process takes about four minutes. The oversized 14.00x20 tires provide better flotation in soft soils. *MFG*

This BMY-built M945A2 used the same 215-inch wheelbase chassis as the M927 and M928, and mounts the generator units for a Patriot missile system. The noise from these units is deafening, and they are usually further from the launch vehicle than this one, which was being demonstrated at a public school. Note that this vehicle does not have the 14.00R20 super single tires, but still relies on 14.00x20s all around, with duals on the tandem bogie to handle the extra weight. Nearly 24,000 M900A2 series trucks were built between 1987 and 1993, and most are still in service.

This version of BMY's M939A2 series trucks was first displayed in 1991, but has never been put into series production. It mounts a 2,000-gallon stainless steel tanker and pump assembly, and could be used either for petroleum or fresh water. The rear-mounted pump module is the same as that used on the M978 HEMMT tanker, with a variable flow rate from 50 to 300 gallons per minute. The GVW was 41,910 pounds, with the truck weighing 27,510 unladen. Plans are under-way to rebuild the durable M900A2 series trucks, at a cost about two-thirds the price of new vehicles. *MFG*

The Tactical Truck Corporation's candidate for the 5-ton 6x6 in the Family of Military Tactical Vehicles (FMTV) program was this low silhouette model. Built by General Motors and BMY as a joint venture, it was one of several TTC

models that was offered for test and evaluation under a 1988 contract. Cummins' 6CTA8.3 inline six-cylinder diesel was used, rated at 300 horsepower in this six wheel version. As with the 2 1/2-ton 4x4, it featured a modular power pack with the engine and Allison seven-speed transmission with integral transfer case, and modular cooling system as well. The driver could see the road only 9 feet ahead of the vehicle, and the cab tilted for routine maintenance. Note the self-loading crane mounted at the rear. *WES*

Teledyne Continental submitted this 5-ton 6x6 as their proposal for the FMTV program, and it too, shared major components with its 2 1/2-ton 4x4 sister. A Caterpillar Model 3116 inline six-cylinder diesel was fitted, coupled to a ZF seven-speed automatic transmission and a two-speed transfer case with a full engine power PTO. This was one of the 15 trucks contracted for in 1988 for test and evaluation, and it had "portal" axles to give better ground clearance, an adjustable air suspension system, which would allow it to be lowered enough to go into cargo aircraft without removing the cab. *TAC*

Of course, when Stewart & Stevenson won the contract for the FMTV in October 1991, it included both the 2 1/2-ton 4x4 and the 5-ton 6x6, and an early production version of the M1083 without winch is seen here. The contract was for 11,000 trucks and was worth $1.2 billion with the trucks being built in Sealy, Texas, near Houston, and production scheduled for late 1992, with the first issue to troops in 1995. There is a 90 percent parts commonality between the 4x4 and 6x6 types. *MFG*

The instrument panel of the new M1000 series FMTV is a far cry from the crude and vertical dashboard in the older M939 series trucks. Even the steering wheel is dished for the safety of the driver, and all switches are close to hand. The driver's view of the road is immensely improved, with the ability to see the pavement about 12 feet in front of the bumper. The steering wheel even has a tilt feature, and there is four cubic feet of storage behind each seat. A middle seat on the engine housing allows for a third passenger.

The M1084 from Stewart & Stevenson is shown here near Swan Creek at Aberdeen Proving Ground, Maryland, with its self-loading crane elevated and the outriggers down for stabilization. With the crane stowed, it is lower than the top edge of the cargo bed sides. The crane can lift 2,500 pounds extended to 14 feet, or 5,000 pounds when retracted to only 7 feet, and it can rotate 360 degrees. It can be controlled both at the base and remotely by cable. *JS*

The M1086 is the long wheelbase version of the new FMTV series, with a 216.5-inch wheelbase and a cargo bed, which is over 20 feet long. The sides of the bed are hinged to drop down for easy loading by a forklift. If a self-recovery winch had been included, it would have been mounted amidships just behind the fuel tank, with fairleads at the front and rear of the truck. The spare tire can be pivoted over onto the ground, simplifying tire changes. The long wheelbase cargo without crane is the M1085. *MFG*

This is the M1088 tractor, which can handle a 25,000-pound payload on the fifth wheel, and tow 60,700 pounds on a semi-trailer. As with the other 6x6 models by Stewart & Stevenson, it uses a Caterpillar Model 3116 turbocharged and air-to-air aftercooled diesel engine, with 290 horsepower from 6.6 liters (403 ci) displacement. It develops 732 foot-pounds of torque at 2,600 rpm. The transmission is an Allison MD-D7 automatic with seven forward speeds, and an integral transfer case with full-time all wheel drive. *MFG*

Although this does not resemble the typical commercial wrecker, the M1089 is the 5-ton wrecker in the FMTV line. With a curb weight of 34,573 pounds, the main recovery winch has a 60,000-pound line pull capacity, while the lifting equipment at the rear has an 11,000-pound capacity, and can be operated from the truck or remotely by cable. The lifting crane is mounted just ahead of the tandem set, and it has a lift capability of 5,000 pounds. The 15,500-pound self-recovery winch is mounted just to the rear of the fuel tank. *JS*

This M1090 was an early dump truck, coming off of the assembly line in February 1995. It has a 5-cubic-yard body, which can handle 10,000 pounds and can tilt to 70 degrees, with operation from inside the cab. The M1090 can be fitted with the 15,500-pound self-recovery winch, which carries 280 feet of steel cable. All 6x6 models have a Rockwell R-611 Type 1 front axle, with a Type 3 and Type 4 for the tandem, except for the M1089 and M1088, which use Rockwell's Type 5 and Type 6 versions. All are single reduction with a planetary set in the hub. The overall axle gear ratio is 7.8:1.

The M1091 fuel tanker is just now being shipped to the active army in 1998, being one of the last to enter production. With an empty weight of 24,194 pounds, it has a GVW in excess of 30,000 pounds when the stainless steel tank is loaded with 1,500 gallons of fuel. It can self-load at 200 gallons per minute, bottom load at 600 gallons per minute, or dispense fuel at 20 to 100 gallons per minute using two 50-foot hoses on reels. The commonality of parts between the 4x4 and 6x6 FMTV models includes the engine (except injectors, turbocharger, and exhaust manifold), along with the entire drive train except for the rear axles, which do vary. The suspensions, steering, and cab assemblies are also interchangeable. *MFG*

Another of the last models to reach the troops is this M1087 expansible van, mounted on a 216-inch wheelbase. Weighing 28,647 pounds empty, it is second only to the M1089 wrecker in curb weight. As with the other 6x6 models, it can tow a 21,000-pound trailer with the pintle hook provided at the rear. The expansible van is 8 feet wide, and is a full 14 feet wide with the sides out. The van module is also designed to be easily removed, and can be placed on the ground if required. *MFG*

This M1093 is the air drop version, being prepared for a parachute trip from a C-130. The roof has been removed and is strapped to the cargo in the bed, and the windows and windshield are folded over the sides and front, respectively. The truck is securely strapped to an aluminum pallet, with layers of honeycomb material fitted tightly under the chassis. This variant weighs 20,278 pounds empty. They are designed either for high altitude drops, or to withstand a low altitude (LAPES) drop. *RW*

Only three of the FMTV trucks are modified for airdrop, the 4x4 M1081 and the 6x6 M1093 (both cargo versions), and this M1094 dump. The cab guard is removable, along with the cab roof, and the sides of the cab fold down, giving a total height of 8 feet 9 inches when prepared for air drop. In the air drop mode, the M1094 would weigh 21,290 pounds without fuel. The dump body had provisions for the installation of troop seats, and for a tarpaulin cover so it could serve as a cargo truck.

This is AM General's Extended Service Program 5-ton 6x6 of 1998. Details of the upgrade have not been released.

3 1/2-Ton 8x8

The Standard Manufacturing Company of Dallas, Texas, has marketed their Trailing Arm Drive (TAD) independent suspension systems for several years, and has applied that system to some vehicles built under their own name. This was their Medium Combat Truck from 1985, which had a top speed of more than 55 miles per hour relying on hydrostatic drive and brakes. With a GVW of 20,000 pounds, 7,000 of which was payload, it was powered by a Cummins 6BT5.9, which was a six-cylinder diesel, with 160 horsepower at 2,800 rpm. The hydraulic suspension could be raised and lowered a total of 8 inches, and the hydrostatic drive had four speed ranges. The tires were 14-17.5, and the truck could handle a 60-percent grade, or a 30-percent side slope. *MFG*

10-Ton 8x8

The Army had experimented with some very large 8x8 cargo trucks, including the XM409 of 1957, the XM977 of 1978, and a few shop-built models. It even had a fleet of Ford 5-ton 8x8s known as the M656, which were transporters for the Pershing missile systems of the 1960s. There was a need for a Heavy Expanded Mobility Tactical Truck (HEMTT), and in 1981, a contract went to Oshkosh for the M977 series truck. One of the pre-production prototypes was this M985E1, which had a very tall HIAB Model 8108 materials handling crane at the rear, with its own outriggers. There was a provision for lowering the crane into the cargo bed for air transport. There are now about 14,000 HEMTTs serving with the Army. *BK*

The production models had a more practical self-loader crane, which folded neatly at the rear of the bed. This early production M977 had a Grove crane capable of lifting 2,500 pounds at the maximum boom length of 19 feet. The truck had a GVW of 62,000 pounds and was powered by a Detroit Diesel 8V92TA engine, which was a 736-ci (12.06 liters) displacement V-8 that gave 445 horsepower and 1,250 foot-pounds of torque at 2,100 rpm. This engine is used in all models of the M977 series, as is Allison's HT740D four-speed automatic transmission with torque converter. An Oshkosh air-operated two-speed transfer is also used. *JS*

The fuel tanker on the Oshkosh 8x8 chassis was the M978, capable of carrying 2,500 gallons of fuel in its stainless steel tank. It had a manhole for gravity fill at the top, or had a 300 gallons per minute suction pump for bottom fill. The curb weight was 36,000 pounds, which went to 36,900 pounds if the mid-ship, 20,000-pound capacity self-recovery winch was fitted. All models except the M984 wrecker used Oshkosh 46K single reduction axles on the steering front tandem with an inter-axle differential and final ratio of 5.57:1. The rear axles were Eaton DS-381 models, which had the same characteristics but did not steer.

There are two versions of the Oshkosh tractor, this M983 without a crane, and a M983 that had an amidships MHE crane along with a self-contained auxiliary generator. This M983 was equipped with the 20,000-pound self-recovery winch with 200 feet of wire rope. The cabs of all models are identical, are steel, capable of carrying two persons, and do not have a tilt feature. The spare 16.00R20 tire is mounted behind the cab on the right, and the air intake is on the left. This trailer on this unit was a Patriot launch unit and had its own generator equipment mounted up on the gooseneck.

This is an early production M984 wrecker, which had a large cargo box in the center, with the main winch behind the crane assembly at the rear of the chassis. The crane is folded down in this view, leaving the spare tire as the highest point on the truck. The 20,000-pound self-recovery winch is mounted just ahead of the forward rear axle. *JS*

An early reconfiguring of the wrecker produced the M984E1, see here from above. This view shows the cab with radiator air intake in the roof, engine cover and air cleaner, spare tire, and hydraulic reservoir at the front. In the midsection are the DP 60,000 pound recovery winch, storage cabinets, oxygen and acetylene bottles, and the 154-gallon fuel tank under the deck. At the rear are the outriggers, folded Grove MHC984 14,000-pound material handling crane, and the vehicle retrieval assembly extended beyond the frame. The curb weight is 50,900 pounds, and the GVW is 95,000 pounds. *JS*

The M985 is the heaviest of the cargo types in the Oshkosh 8x8 series, with a curb weight of 39,600 pounds and a GVW of 68,000 pounds. The self-loading crane is a Grove MHC985, and it can lift 5,400 pounds when extended to the maximum 16.5 feet. The cargo bed sides fold down for loading by forklift. As with all of these Oshkosh models, the ground clearance is 24 inches, and the maximum fording depth is 48 inches. Angles of approach and departure are 41 and 45 degrees respectively. They can climb a 60-percent grade, and run on a 30-percent side slope.

This Oshkosh is the 10-ton HEMTT-LHS, which uses a Mark V Multilift (Modified) as the load handler. The hydraulic boom is seen at the rear preparing to bring the pallet aboard for transport. Four of these LHS models have been built for evaluation by the Army. They weigh 36,600 pounds and can be airlifted in a C-130. The total GVW is 61,000 pounds. A Simula armored cab has been fitted to this particular truck: all external metal surfaces have been protected by light armor plate, and there is a baffle assembly covering the front air intake. Clear ballistic material is used in the windshield and door windows, and to cover the headlamps.

In the fall of 1983, Oshkosh got the contract to build 1,433 of the Marine Corps' Mk 48 Logistical Vehicle System (LVS) trucks. It was derived from the earlier Lockheed Dragon Wagon and was articulated behind the power unit, allowing 32 degrees of yaw steering right or left, and 6 degrees of roll either way. This allowed the turning radius to be

the same as its length: 38 feet. Four versions were offered: this flatbed container carrier (Mk 48/14), a recovery vehicle (Mk 48/15), tractor (Mk 48/16), and dropside cargo truck (Mk 48/17). The payload of the Mk 48 is 12.5 tons off-road and 22.5 tons on surfaced roads. The Marines now have about 1,700 LVSs. *JS*

The Mk 48 is engineered as a multi-module truck, with the power unit able to drop off one trailer module and go out for another. Once decoupled, the rear unit rests on landing gear. All variants use a 445-horsepower Detroit Diesel 8V92TA engine with 736-ci displacement. There is a four-speed Allison

HT740D automatic transmission with torque converter and a Oshkosh two-speed transfer case. These are housed in the front unit, along with the two front drive/steering axles. The rear unit is driven by a propshaft from the front module. The tires are 16.00R21. *MFG*

There are two articulated elements on this Mk 48: the tractor itself bends in the middle, and the semi-trailer is mounted on the fifth wheel. The tractor is shorter, with a 229-inch wheelbase, while the other versions have a 259-inch wheelbase. The first steering axle is an Oshkosh with an inter-axle differential, the second steering axle is an Eaton RS-381 with wheel-to-wheel differential. The tandem rear axles are Eaton DS-580 types with inter-axle and wheel-to-wheel differentials. The box on the roof of this truck is the cab air conditioner. *MFG*

The Army's Family of Heavy Tactical Vehicles included 10-ton 8x8 trucks, which were to be used in the Army's general support rocket system (GSRS). M-A-N, of West Germany, built a fleet of tractors (XM1001) and wreckers (XM1002) around 1981 that carried the Pershing missile systems based in Europe. By 1986, GMC was working with M-A-N and offered this vehicle as the transporter for the Pershings, and for the new Patriot missile system then being fielded. The American version was to have U.S. components rather than the German components found in the earlier M-A-N trucks. *MFG*

Oshkosh became the builder of the trucks for the Patriot system, and in 1989, General Motors offered this revamped version of the M-A-N/GMC as a candidate for the Palletized Loading System (PLS) for the Army. It used a Detroit Diesel 8V92TA engine with 500 horsepower, and an Allison CLT-754 five-speed transmission and Rockwell T-2214 transfer. The Eaton axles were to be made under license from M-A-N, with planetary gear sets out in the hubs. A Grove material handling crane was used, and they would build the load handling system under license from Bennes Marrel of France. Perhaps only this prototype was assembled, as the contract for the PLS went to Oshkosh. *MFG*

25-Ton 8x8

In the summer of 1988, the competition for the Army's new Heavy Equipment Transporter (HET) was intensifying, and AM General displayed their "M1A1 Hauler." It was a relatively conventional machine, with the big diesel engine mounted out in front of the driver, but with a sloping hood for better visibility. An 8x8, it had twin steering axles under the engine compartment, and another tandem set under the fifth wheel. Steering axles on the trailer would help the unit work its way through the often narrow village streets of central Europe. Technical details were never released, as the Oshkosh M1070 was soon selected for production. *MFG*

The Oshkosh M1070 prototypes were ready for testing in the fall of 1990, with production set for spring 1992. More than 1,500 have been built, all using Detroit Diesel's 8V-92TA, which developed 500 horsepower, working with an Allison five-speed transmission and the Oshkosh 55000 series two-speed transfer. All axles were Rockwell Model SVI 5MR series, with planetary reduction gears out in the hub and differential locks on the tridem, with the first and fourth axles steering. The huge cab will carry five fully equipped troops, helping to bring the GVW to 87,000 pounds. The curb weight was 41,000 pounds. An M88A1 tank retriever is on the trailer in this view.

This Oshkosh M1070 has just been delivered to Fort Knox and still has its ancillary equipment crated and banded to the fifth wheel. The main winches sit above the first axle of the tridem, and are DP Manufacturing's Model 55K. Each is operated by a two-speed hydraulic motor, and has a 55,000 pound capacity, with 170 feet of 1-inch wire rope. A 3,000-pound auxiliary DP Model 3GN winch is also amidships, with a single-speed hydraulic motor. It is used to pull the steel rope from the main winches back to the

vehicle to be towed. The M1070 has a central tire inflation system, which is operated from the cab. It carries 250 gallons of fuel and runs on 16.00R20 super single tires all around.

The PLS is intended primarily for artillery units, so they can handle ammunition in large quantities. About 3,400 PLS trucks were to be built, freeing earlier HEMMTs to be reassigned to armor, mechanized infantry, and aviation units. But while the chassis was intended for cargo pallets, other modules can be applied equally well. One of the recent efforts is this fuel or water module, which

can be off-loaded quickly and has its own one-cylinder diesel engine to power the 50 to 300 gallons per minute pump. The 3,000-gallon tank is of stainless steel and has just one compartment with a single manhole in the top. *MFG*

Another variant on the PLS system by Oshkosh is this 12- to 14-cubic yard dump truck that employs a single telescopic hydraulic cylinder to elevate the body. It was assembled in 1997 as a working prototype for evaluation by the U.S. military. It has the same engine and drive train as the basic PLS chassis: an electronically controlled Detroit Diesel Model 8V92TA engine, with 500 horsepower from 736 inches of displacement in a V-8 configuration. The peak torque is 1,470 foot-pounds at 1,200 rpm. Allison's Model CLT-755 ATEC five-speed automatic torque converter transmission is used, with an Oshkosh two-speed planetary transfer with differential lock. *MFG*

Oshkosh has also placed a maintenance module on the chassis of the PLS 10x10 truck as an experimental unit. As a self-contained maintenance and repair shop, it contains its own generator, air compressor, hydraulic pump, self-loading crane, and the infinite number of tools and fixtures needed to maintain a fleet of tanks or trucks. As with the other base and variant models, the tires are 16.00R20 Michelin XZLT types, and there is a central tire inflation system. All axles are Rockwell SVI 5MR planetary hub models, each with a 26,455-pound rating, with steering on the front tandem set and the final axle in the tridem. *MFG*

CHAPTER SIX

SPECIALIZED WHEELED VEHICLES

The weird, peculiar, odd, and esoteric vehicles that are used by the U.S. military are so numerous it is hard to know where to begin, and sometimes it is difficult to know just how to categorize them.

All of the services use highly specialized machines. There are very light, high-speed, fat-tired sand runners. There are angular, amphibious armored cars for urban warfare, immense lattice boom cranes for use on the ocean, and vehicles that sniff for chemicals. We've had tractor trailers that looked like a frog in the sand, and trucks that spray deicing fluid on a cold airplane just before a very small truck appears to start that airplane. These are included here, and many more besides.

The military services often have a difficult time persuading the bureaucrats that their specialized vehicles are even needed. There is a mind-set that says one type of tow truck should serve everyone's needs, or perhaps even that some of the services these vehicles render could be done without. But when the emergency arises, the only thing that can pick up a burning aircraft and move it to a safe location is a huge crane that can move pretty quickly for short distances. The only thing that can move across desert sands at night, quietly, carrying a team of three, accomplish its mission, and return safely to base is a dune buggy, even if it doesn't look very military.

These vehicles often not only do not look very military, some of them are downright strange. But they serve useful purposes, like having the responsibility for sniffing bacteriological or chemical agents. Or for providing armor protection for a maintenance team moving into the line of fire to recover crew on a vehicle that cannot move without help. Or for spreading thousands of gallons of water on a hot, dry assembly area so the troops don't have to choke on the dust. When you see them doing what they are designed to do, they don't look so strange anymore.

Chenowth built 80 of these Fast Attack Vehicles for the Army, and by the time this one got to Fort Knox for evaluation in the summer of 1984, it had acquired a formidable appearance, even if it was only 60 inches high at the cal.50 machine gun. Wire baskets had been added between the wheels to carry gear, and the headlamps are out where they can stay cleaner. The VW-based air-cooled engine was still used, along with a synchronized four-speed transmission and 5.4:1 rear axle ratio. All mechanical components had been extensively strengthened for military use. Note the radio set behind the seats. Much to the delight of the operators, this rig had seen some very hard test miles. *AEB*

FAST ATTACK AND LIGHT STRIKE VEHICLES

When the Army started working with dune buggies as scout and reconnaissance vehicles, they still looked like a typical dune buggy. This photo was taken at Fort Lewis, Washington, in 1982, and shows a clean, lithe machine with minimal modifications for the military. They were originally evaluated by the 9th Infantry Division at Fort Lewis, and of several manufacturers who supplied prototypes, only those by Chenowth of El Cajon, California, completed all tests and were available to the Army on schedule. The Chenowth FAV completed one test course in 9.5 minutes, while a HMMWV took 16 minutes and a tracked M113A1 took a half-hour. The engine was a 94-horsepower modified four-cylinder VW with air-cooling and was mounted at the extreme rear, where it gave better traction for the rear-drive buggy. *ARMY*

The weapons mount could also be placed on the cowl of the 1,570-pound Chenowth FAV, allowing the gunner to keep a much lower profile. The frame was tubular, and there were two high performance shock absorbers at each front wheel, three at each rear wheel. The wheelbase was 103 inches, and the tire sizes were 7.00x15 front and 10.15 rear. The top speed was 70 to 80 miles per hour, with a 0-60 time under 12 seconds with 480 pounds aboard. The FAV is designed to operate for several hours away from base; the heavier Light Strike Vehicles are able to operate for several days. To date, Chenowth has built well over 300 FAVs, about half of which are with the Army. *MFG*

The Fredericksburg, Virginia, firm NORDAC offered their Model NMC-40 Long Range Fast Attack Vehicle around 1983, but they were not produced in series. It featured an interesting seating arrangement, with the driver and assistant facing forward with one machine gun, and a third occupant facing the rear with another weapon. The NMC-40 used a VW 1, 800-cc four-cylinder air-cooled engine, and a VW Type 2 four-speed transaxle, both heavily modified. Disc brakes were mounted on the rear, which could be operated independently for tight turns. *MFG*

Teledyne Continental Motors built two of their Light Forces Vehicle (LFV) around 1985. It was low, at 62 inches, reducible to 53 inches for air transport, weighed 2,500 pounds net, and could carry a 1,600-pound payload A 115-horsepower engine was fitted, with a three-speed automatic transmission, along with disc brakes all around and full-time four-wheel drive with limited slip differentials and air suspension. The turbocharged diesel gave 0-30 acceleration in 4.5 seconds, and 70 miles per hour top speed. Sitting on a 115-inch wheelbase, it used 7.50x16XS tires. The LFV is seen here with a TOW missile launcher mounted on the roof. *MFG*

The competitors gone, the Lockheed-Martin Chenowth has become the FAV of choice U.S. military. This three-man machine has been purchased by both the Army and the Navy's SEALs, where it is known as the Desert Patrol Vehicle (DPV). The gunner sits high and to the rear. The Marines also got eight of these for use in Desert Storm, and refer to them as Light Strike Vehicles (LSV). The side racks normally carry supplies and gear but can be used as emergency litters. This vehicle still relies on a militarized VW engine and powertrain. *MFG*

In the fall of 1996, Chenowth displayed their Advanced Light Strike Vehicle, a four-man, four-wheel drive model that can operate for prolonged periods with minimal support. It has a 125-horsepower five-cylinder water-cooled diesel, a five-speed transmission, and can move from 0 to 60 in 20 seconds, with a top speed well over 70 miles per hour. The GVW is 5,170 pounds, and it can climb a 60-percent slope or traverse a 40-percent slope. Weaponry would include a M2-caliber .50 machine gun or the MK 19 grenade launcher, along with light machine guns. *MFG*

One of the latest offerings by Lockheed Martin-Chenowth is this GP (General Purpose) vehicle, derived from an earlier RAMP (Rapid Multipurpose Vehicle) by TPC Logistics Services of Farmingdale, NY. It has now been upgraded with 2.6-liter four-cylinder militarized Volkswagen engine and a heavy-duty four-speed transmission. The wheelbase is 112 inches, it is 168 inches long, and is capable of carrying 6 to 8 troops with a GVW of 4,620 pounds. Its configuration allows it to also be adapted for use as an ambulance. The GPV is being built for the U.S. Navy. *MFG*

Chenowth's Light Strike Vehicle is still in production, and this latest edition of the LSV is for the Marines. It is 161 inches long and 79 inches high, with a ground clearance of 16 inches. The GVW is 3,160 pounds, and it is on a 112-inch wheelbase. The 2.2-liter four-cylinder air-cooled engine gives 125 horsepower, and the top speed is around 75 miles per hour. It can climb a 75-percent grade, and cruise over 300 miles. These LSVs can also be ordered with light protective armor, an all weather package, communications equipment, and with a variety of weapons mounts. *MFG*

Land Rovers are not often found in the vehicle inventory of the U.S. military, and the few we have are rarely seen. In 1992, 60 of these were provided to the Special Forces, where they serve as long range reconnaissance vehicles for special missions. Based on Land Rover's Defender 110 series, it uses a 3.5-liter V-8 diesel of 134 horsepower, working with a manual five-speed transmission and two-speed transfer. The roll bars at the rear have weapons mounts on them, and another machine gun is mounted on the dashboard. There are provisions to carry a mortar and anti-tank missile launcher, and there are stowage compartments for mines, demolition gear and the crew's personal items. *ARMY*

ARMORED CARS

Rarely seen and little discussed, this unusual armored car was built by the Hendrickson Manufacturing Company of Lyons, Illinois, and was provided to Argentina around 1975. It was sold as a kit, to be applied to a normal all-wheel-drive three axle truck chassis. Primarily intended for riot control, the driver could elevate and use the windshield, or depress and use periscopes for visibility. There was no cover provided over the troop compartment in the kit, but that could have easily been added later. *MFG*

This Bell Aerospace Hydracobra was introduced around 1984, reflecting an agreement between Bell and ENGESA of Brazil to assemble these vehicles in the United States using primarily American-built components. It was intended to compete for the Army and Marine's Light Armored Vehicle (LAV) program. A Detroit Diesel 6V53N or T model was anticipated for use, working with an Allison MT-643 four-speed automatic transmission. The front axle had independent suspension, while the rear tandem used ENGESA's walking beam system. When GM's 8x8 Bison was accepted as the new LAV, the Bell-ENGESA project was abandoned. *MFG*

In 1984, Emergency One, a manufacturer of fire apparatus in Ocala, Florida, announced their Mk44 armored car. Intended for use as a personnel carrier or as a weapons platform, it featured a Deutz air-cooled diesel with 256 horse-power at 2,650 rpm. With a curb weight of 20,400 pounds, it had good armor protection while still offering acceleration from 0-45 miles per hour in 24 seconds, and a top speed of 65 miles per hour. A four-speed powershift transmission with integral transfer case was used, and 47 gallons of fuel allowed more than 700 miles of travel. With a height of 7 feet 8 inches, it was relatively low, but still had an amphibious capability with no preparation needed to swim. A six wheel version was also offered. *MFG*

El Salvador had a need for light armor protection for their armed forces, but could not afford purpose-built armored cars. They did have a fleet of 1950s Dodge 3/4-ton M37 4x4 trucks, and the Army's Tank Automotive Command responded by building kits that the Salvadorans could install on their old trucks. The kits were partially assembled, with all esoteric welding done at TACOM, then shipped to El Salvador for final welding and assembly. A total of 66 trucks were so modified, and the armor was tested for protection from 5.56-millimeter ball ammunition, sufficient for the type of opposition found in El Salvador. *GP*

The Dragoon 300 series armored car was built at Southfield, Michigan, by the Arrowpointe Corporation. It was initially designed to meet an Army Military Police requirement, and used major components from the M809 series 5-ton truck and the M113A2 APC. It was a monocoque design made of high hardness ballistic steel plate, with the driver at the left front. Side doors are provided between the axles, and the engine is at the right rear. Used in limited quantities by the Army and Navy, it had a 300-horsepower Detroit Diesel 6V53T engine, Allison MT-653DR five-speed transmission, single-speed transfer, and 14.00x20 tires. It was amphibious, moving through the water by spinning its wheels. *MFG*

Cadillac Gage has built their Commando Scout since 1978, and it is still on the market. A relatively small vehicle at 16,500 pounds, it carries a crew of two or three, and has a top speed of 60 miles per hour and a range of over 800 miles on 100 gallons of fuel. The engine is a Cummins V-6 diesel with 149 horsepower, and it is teamed with an Allison four-speed automatic transmission and two-speed transfer. It has single reduction axles with locking differentials, coil springs all around, and the tires are 14.5R20. *MFG*

The Cadillac Gage Commando 150 is derived from the V-100 (M706) of the 1970s, and is now known as the LAV-150 ST. The new variant now has a Cummins 6CTA 8.3 turbocharged and aftercooled inline six-cylinder diesel, with 250 horsepower at 2,500 rpm from 8.3 liters displacement. An Allison six-speed automatic works with a single speed transfer case, and the axles are double reduction types with locking differentials. With solid axles and leaf springs, it is fully amphibious, using the spinning wheels for movement and turning, and it has a GVW of 24,000 pounds. The LAV-150 ST can mount a variety of weapons, from a 7.62-millimeter machine gun to a 90-millimeter cannon. *MFG*

AM General's HMMWV suspension is used on the monocoque body of this armored car. It is built in Turkey by Otokar, and exported as required by AM General. Intended primarily as a convoy escort or perimeter security vehicle, it has been designated as the Light Armored Squad Carrier, and it has armor on all sides and the bottom capable of withstanding 7.62 armor piercing ammunition, 12-pound land mines, and artillery air bursts. For its own protection, the turret can be fitted with a weapon up to cal.50. Run-flat tires are part of the package, along with the GM 5.6-liter diesel engine found in the heavy HMMWV variants. *MFG*

Cadillac Gage has built their six wheel models since 1983, and have been known as the V-300, V-300A1, and currently as the LAV-300, generally with smaller caliber weapons mounted. With the same general appearance as the LAV-300, this new LAV-600 is the successor to the V-600 of the late 1980s, and it can easily handle the 105-millimeter low recoil gun system mounted in this view. It has Cadillac Gage's gyro stabilization system and can fire on the move with excellent accuracy. A 275-horsepower Cummins 6CTA8.3 engine is used, along with a six-speed Allison automatic transmission, two-speed transfer, and single reduction axles with differential locks. The suspension and hull construction are the same as the LAV-300, but the total GVW of the LAV-600 is 40,700 pounds. *MFG*

The American military has evaluated various nuclear, biological, and chemical (NBC) detection systems for years, but did not get serious about a vehicle-mounted system until the Gulf War. Since there was insufficient time to field a home-grown version, 60 examples of an existing system built by the German firm Thyssen-Henschel were brought into action, and they performed extremely well. From that auspicious start, the Army now has about 300 of them. A three-person crew operates the M93 "Fox," monitoring their immediate environment using small wheels that run along the ground and an air sampler. Traces are immediately analyzed by an on-board mass

spectrometer. Operators then mark the contaminated areas, and advise nearby units of NBC contamination by radio. *AFCC*

This M93 Fox was loaned by the German government for Desert Storm, and shows the propellers that enable it to move and turn quickly in the water. The vehicles bought after Desert Storm have air conditioning and special provisions for American weapons and smoke grenade launchers, along with a position/navigation system, and can be operated for 12 hours without resupply. The gross weight is 37,400 pounds, and it uses a Mercedes-Benz OM 402A turbocharged, liquid-cooled V-8 diesel with 320 horsepower at 2,500 rpm, and a six-speed ZF Model 6HP 500 automatic transmission with torque converter. It steers on the front two axles, and uses 14.00x20 tires. *AD*

In the search for a Light Armored Vehicle (LAV) to support the Marines and the Army Light Infantry Divisions, vehicles from Alvis, Cadillac Gage, and GM of Canada were evaluated. The GM product referred to as the Bison became the choice of both services. It had excellent mobility thanks to eight 11.00x16 tires with independent suspension all around,

coil springs on the front steering axles, and torsion bars on the rear two axles. It could be operated as an 8x4 or as an 8x8, and was amphibious. This Infantry Section Carrier is one of the more recent versions, and it can carry eight combat-ready troops. *MFG*

The initial contract for the General Motors LAV was for 969 vehicles, mostly for the Army. However, the Army's participation was eliminated in 1984 due to the use of HMMWVs and a decision by Congress to cancel funds. Hence, the only LAVs in the American military are in the Marine Corps, and they initially bought 758 of them, including this early Command and Control version, plus a 25-millimeter cannon type, the TOW missile carrier, mortar carrier, maintenance and recovery rig, and a logistics carrier. The LAV-C (command and control) is turretless, and carries radio and communications equipment. *JS*

The Swiss firm MOWAG was the initial designer of the LAV, and they marketed 4x4, 6x6, and 8x8 versions under the name Piranha. General Motors of Canada subsequently teamed with MOWAG to build Americanized versions in North America. All of the Marine Corps vehicles use a Detroit Diesel 6V53T turbocharged V-6 engine, with 275 horsepower at 2,800 rpm, and it works with an Allison MT 653 automatic five-speed transmission and a transfer case. This is the Mobile Electronic Warfare Support System (MEWSS) variant, which is capable of two-way communication, data collection, pinpointing enemy units, and jamming and intercepting communications. *MFG*

The LAV was quickly adapted to carry the TOW missile system, and this one was operating in Saudi Arabia during Desert Storm in 1991. Owned by the Marines, it has been painted sand beige and is heavily laden with crew gear, C-rations, jerry cans, and a spare tire. As with all the others, it steers on the two front axles, and all axles have a planetary gearset in the outer hubs. There were 50 of this TOW anti-tank version in the original order, and it is the improved TOW Under Armor, built by Emerson Electric. The launcher rotates 360 degrees, and can elevate -30 degrees to +34 degrees, and can fire all versions of the TOW missile. Two missiles are carried in the launcher; 14 more are stored under armor. *AFCC*

The latest variant of the LAV to enter production is this air defense system, which uses General Electric's Blazer system. This employs eight Stinger missiles in two pods, or can attack with the rapid-fire GAU-12/U 25mm Gatling gun, which can fire at the rate of 2,200 shots per minute. It also employs a forward-looking infrared targeting sight and a laser rangefinder. A total of 17 of these were delivered in the spring of 1998; the first LAVs purchased since the 758 were originally bought in 1984. *MFG*

The LAV-25 was one of the types initially purchased by the Marines, and they have served well. It mounts a single barrel M242 25-millimeter Bushmaster chain gun as the primary weapon, and a M240 7.62-millimeter machine gun as the secondary. Smoke grenade launchers are mounted at the front corners of the turret. This LAV-25 has a quick sand camouflage paint job for Desert Storm. All LAVs are amphibious, and can swim by simply lowering the trim vane and shifting the transfer case. There are four rudders and two propellers, and the drive options are 8x4 or 8x8 on land or water drive. *MFG*

This is the LAV-M or Mortar Carrier. It has a large double folding door hatch in the center of the roof, with a rotating platform on the hull floor to allow the M252 81-millimeter mortar to rotate for aiming. Ninety mortar rounds are stored in the left rear. The mortar can also be removed and fired from its ground mount. As with the other models, this mortar LAV is equipped with a fire suppression system in both the crew and engine compartments, using Halon 1301 as the extinguishing agent. For operating when buttoned up, the driver has three M17 periscopes and one night vision device, and the vehicle commander has similar equipment. *MFG*

The LAV-R is the Mobile Repair Team Vehicle, and it has the capability of recovering vehicles of its size or smaller, and has a 30,000 pound recovery winch at the rear and an A-frame for stabilization. The boom has a 265-degree traverse and is rated at 9,000 pounds when using the outriggers mounted at the center between the third and fourth tires. The LAV-R is also equipped with two welders, a 10,000 watt generator, and an extendible workbench. As with all other models, it also has a self-recovery winch and an NBC protection system.
MFG

The LAVs were 21 feet long, 8 feet 4 inches high at the hull roof, and 8 feet 2 inches wide. They had a road speed of 62 miles per hour, and most weighed around 19,000 pounds net and could carry a 7,000-pound payload. They could swim at 6 miles per hour, climb a 70-percent grade, and run on a 35-percent side slope. The travel range was 485 miles on surfaced roads. This Logistics Carrier (LAV-L) had no turret, but featured a large hatch in the roof and a small jib boom for loading supplies. MFG

At the other extreme from the little truck with a Gatling Gun is this true giant. It was the test bed for the Hardened Mobile Launcher (HML) that was to carry the Air Force's Midgetman ICBM. Built by Boeing Aerospace and Goodyear Aerospace, they were to engage in the "mobile basing" program that moved the missiles intermittently and placed them in different underground silos so the enemy could not tell where they were at any given time. The tires had a 54-inch diameter and a 750-horsepower supercharged diesel was in the tractor, with a similar 550-horsepower model at the rear of the trailer, and the trailer had steering. MFG

In an effort to create a look-alike for the Soviet SA-8 air defense missile system, the Army had its Fort Bliss, Texas, shops create this lifelike weapons system simulator known as the XM08S. It was built by Industrial Vehicles International of Tulsa, Oklahoma, on an elongated truck chassis, and is able to move about the desert training areas. Among Soviet equipment, the SA-8 was unique in that it had all elements necessary to locate, track, and engage a target mounted on the single vehicle, and the American version performs the same functions in simulation. *ARMY*

When the Midgetman ICBM Hard Mobile Launcher was approved (a tracked competitor lost the bid), the camouflaged pre-production prototype by Boeing/Loral looked like a huge reptile. The total length was 105 feet, the height was 10 feet 6 inches, with the trailer only 7 feet high when lowered. The tractor was 12 feet wide, the trailer 14 feet wide. The total weight was 242,000 pounds, with 63,000 of that being the tractor, 179,000 the loaded launcher. A single Rolls-Royce/Perkins 1,200-horsepower turbocharged diesel was used, along with a six-speed electro-hydraulic shift transmission. The top speed was 55 miles per hour. The Midgetman missile program was canceled, and the truck was never used. *VV*

Liftking of Woodbridge, Ontario, has provided several types of rough terrain forklifts to the U.S. Air Force, including this Model LK 1354 of 1991. Shot at Minot AFB, North Dakota, in a setting sun, the all-wheel-drive unit has a height of only 95 inches, with 16.00x25 tires, which are almost 50 inches high themselves. Weighing 29,700 pounds net, it had a 152-horsepower Cummins 6BT5.9 diesel engine, Clark three-speed (forward and reverse) powershift transmission, and Clark No-Spin axles. It could handle a 13,000-pound load, raising it as high as 78 inches.

A newcomer to the military materials handling fleet is the extended-reach fork lift. Numerous makes were tested in the mid-1980s, and Trak International's Sky Trak has provided over 1,600 to the Army to support the MLRS missile system. This is their model 9038, and it can lift 6,000 pounds out to 15 feet, 4,000 pounds to 23 feet. It has two-wheel, four-wheel, and crab steering, a Cummins turbocharged model 6BT5.9 inline six-cylinder engine with 140 horsepower, Funk Model 1723 powershift transmission and Rockwell planetary axles with disc brakes all around. The tires are 17.5x25, and the three-stage boom is hydraulically powered with a 58-gallon reservoir. *MFG*

In 1995, the Entwistle Company of Hudson, Massachusetts, supplied 653 of this 4,400-pound rough terrain forklift to the Army, and they are used extensively for loading aircraft and unstuffing containers, helped by a low (80 inch) silhouette. This is Entwistle's Model 9609, and it uses a Cummins 4B3.9 four-cylinder diesel of 80 horsepower and 3.9 liters displacement. A Clark powershift transmission gave three speeds forward and reverse. It had selective 4x2 or 4x4, and selective two-wheel or four-wheel steer. With a GVW of 12,250 pounds, it ran on 15R19.5 tires.

Forklifts also come in very big sizes, and this 50,000-pound-capacity Caterpillar rough terrain container handler weighs 113,000 pounds when equipped with an adapter to lift 40-foot containers. It is shown here while being transported on a lowboy in the Persian Gulf, and is one of 450 stationed worldwide with the U.S. Army and Marine Corps. A 393-horsepower Caterpillar 3408 engine is used, with a planetary type Caterpillar transmission with torque converter. It has four forward and four reverse speeds. With articulated steering, it also has rear axle oscillation plus or minus 13 degrees, but no suspension. All wheels drive, with a planetary reduction gearset in each wheel, and the tires are 6535x33 steel belted radials. The height is 13 feet 6 inches at the cab roof, and it can wade in 60 inches of salt water. *AFCC*

For medium lifting requirements, the American military has bought large numbers of this 1989 Lorain (Koehring) Model LRT 110, Type I. A very compact little unit, it is only 12 feet high and 26 feet long as seen here, but can extend its boom to 30 feet lifting 4,000 pounds or 15,000 pounds at a 10-foot length, elevate to 75 degrees, and rotate 360

degrees. It is a 4x4 with planetary hubs and offers two-wheel, four-wheel, or crab steer, and it has 15.00x22.5 tires. An 80-horsepower Cummins 4B3.9 four-cylinder diesel is used, with a Funk four-speed (forward and reverse) powershift transmission with torque converter. It has a GVW of 23,870 pounds as a Type I (standard), or 24,230 pounds as the Airmobile Type II.

At the large end of the military crane spectrum is this Grove RT 875 CC rough terrain crane, big enough to lift the average house. With a 70-ton capacity, the three-section boom can extend to 208 feet. Powered by a 250-horsepower Cummins 6CTA8.3 diesel engine, it has a Clark Powershift three-speed two-range transmission (six forward, six reverse) with torque converter and Rockwell planetary axles. The GVW is 94,500 pounds. About 155 were built for the Army, Air Force, and Marine Corps.

Caterpillar's Model 613B Water Distributor Type I is an indispensable vehicle when operating in hot, dry areas. It can carry 2,500 gallons of water at 25 miles per hour across almost any terrain, then spread that water through four adjustable spray heads to reduce dust or to wash off hardstand. Caterpillar's own four-stroke Model 3208 diesel V-8 is used, with 150 horsepower from 636 ci of displacement. A powershift four-speed transmission with torque converter is used, and the drive goes to the planetary geared front axle only. The tires are 18.00x25, and the steering is by hydraulic articulation just behind the cab. Weighing 30,500 pounds, that can be reduced to 29,700 for air drop. *MFG*

This is essentially an Air Force John Deere Model 690C excavator with an undercarriage by Standard Manufacturing of Dallas, TX, and it can be operated either from the armor-plated cab or robotically. It is designed to excavate unexploded ordnance or other hazardous materials, and can dig 20 feet deep. The remote control station has a video feature, so the operator can see what the 690C is doing. The engine is a John Deere 125-horsepower turbocharged diesel, and the hydrostatic drive has variable two-speed hydraulic propelling motors with a two-speed planetary gear reduction to move the chassis. It also has multiple disc brakes. *MFG*

The A/S 32 MB-2 series of Air Force tow tractors has a long history, and the latest models can be rather awesome. Stewart & Stevenson built this version in 1982, and along with being short and squat, it is very heavy at 26 tons. Intended for towing large aircraft, it uses a Detroit Diesel 4V53T that displaces 424 cubic inches (6.95 liters), and has an Allison semi-automatic dual range (four forward, two reverse) torque converter transmission. Steering is by electro-hydraulics with three modes: two wheel, four wheel, or crab. The turning radius is only 12 feet, while the overall length is 17 feet. Limited slip interaxle differentials are by Stewart & Stevenson, and the 13.24:1 axles are by Soma of America.

In the late 1970s, the Air Force gave up using modified farm tractors with cabs as light tow vehicles, and began ordering "bobtail" trucks, known as Flight Line Tow Tractors (FLTT). With a short 87-inch wheelbase and an overall length of 14 feet, it had a 7,400-pound rear axle with a 7.17:1 gear ratio and a 7,100-pound GVW. They are used to move ancillary equipment such as mobile power plants around the airfield. This 1982 version was based on a Ford F-350, and it had a 127-horsepower, 4.9-liter six-cylinder Ford gasoline engine, with Ford's C6 automatic three-speed transmission. The tires were 18.00x16.5, and PSI Mobile Products was the builder of this FLTT II.

Shady Grove, Pennsylvania, is the home of Grove International, and they have built specialized military rigs for decades. This was also an A/S 32 MB-2, built in 1984, with a design unique to Grove. This is the left rear view (it looks similar from the other end), and is available in two models rated at 40,000 pounds or 53,000 pounds capacity. A Cummins 6BT5.9 six-cylinder diesel is packed in the frame, along with a six-speed powershift transmission. It has Rockwell planetary steering axles, and this lighter model runs on 11.00x24 tires. The drawbar pull is 27,000 pounds, at three to four miles per hour.

There have been several purchases of the little "bobtail" tow trucks by the Air Force, including this unusual version built in 1985 by PSI. It was based on the rarely seen AM General CJ-10 1-ton chassis, with rectangular lamps out in the fenders. PSI built 1,500 of these, the first FLTT to have a diesel engine, and it was a 3.5-liter Nissan six cylinder, with a four-speed Chrysler automatic. Weighing 6,000 pounds, it had a load capacity of 1,000 pounds, and a drawbar capacity of 4,000 pounds. The most recent bobtail Flight Line Tow Tractor (FLTT) is a 1997 Dodge Ram model built by Entwistle, 1,054 of which were delivered in 1997.

A commercial attempt to capitalize on the Air Force's requirement for a light flight line vehicle was the Eagle Bobtail, type A/S 32 MB-4, made in Grosse Isle, Michigan. As with many aircraft tugs, the Eagle Bobtail had no suspension system, but it did have four-wheel steer, two-wheel steer, and crab steering (as seen here). It weighed 12,000 pounds, and was based on a 1985 Chevrolet C30, using a Detroit Diesel 6.2-liter V-8 with 135 horsepower, and a Hydramatic Model 400 three-speed transmission with torque converter, with a New Process single-speed transfer. The planetary geared axles were by Zahnradfabrik Friedrichshausen (ZF) and had a 22.02:1 ratio. Four wheel disc brakes operated in oil, and the tires were 8.25x20 with 65 psi.

Stewart & Stevenson built this A/S 32 U-30 for the Air Force in 1987, capable of easily moving the giant C5 Galaxie aircraft. It had 50,000 pounds drawbar pull and a GVW of 63,500 pounds. A turbocharged 318-ci Detroit Diesel 6V53T was fitted, with a ZF 4WG182 automatic transmission and torque converter with four forward speeds, three in reverse. A large DP model 60KS winch is mounted at the rear, with a 60,000-pound capacity using 1-inch steel rope. The tires are Michelin 14.00R24 and the driving axles have planetary gears in the hubs. Rhein-Main AFB, Germany, is the home of this unit.

PSI Mobile Products built these unique MB-4 tugs around 1989, with a little bit of Jeep engineered into the grille. Powered by a Perkins 4.236T turbodiesel with 110 horsepower, it used a three-speed electric shift semi-automatic transmission with transfer case and International Transmission driving axles. The brakes were discs, with four calipers on each front and two calipers on each rear wheel. The tires were 7.50x20, and it had semi-elliptic leaf springs. The drawbar pull was 11,000 pounds, and it could tow 175,000 pounds at 15 miles per hour.

One of the newer A/S 32 MB-2 tug in the Air Force inventory is this Grove model, built in 1995. They look about the same coming or going (this is a rear view), and weighed 40,000 or 53,000 pounds depending on the equipment. On a

120-inch wheelbase, the tires are 12.00x24, and they can handle 14,000 pounds each when inflated to 105 psi. Cummins provided the engine, a 6CT8.3C six-cylinder model with 504 cubic inches displacement. A Clark three-speed long drop transmission with electric shift is used, and the planetary geared axles are by Rockwell. With a drawbar pull of 27,000 pounds, it can travel from 3 to 15 miles per hour.

In 1995, the Air Force acquired some heavy tugs from Jetway Systems of Ogden, Utah. Their B-1000 had the low silhouette of many of the earlier MB-2 models, but incorporated a cab that offered exceptionally good visibility while operating on the flightline. A 260-horsepower Caterpillar Model 3208 provided the power, working with a ZF power-shift four-speed automatic transmission with torque converter and full time four-wheel drive. It had two-wheel, four-wheel, or crab steering. With a GVW of 100,000 pounds, it had a drawbar pull rating of 72,000 pounds.

The Entwistle Company is currently providing this A/S 32 MB-4 to the Air Force and will build 300 of them by 1999. It has a drawbar pull of 14,000 pounds and is classed as a medium capacity unit. A Cummins diesel works with a four-speed automatic transmission, and the four-wheel drive tug can be steered by two wheels, four wheels, or in the crab mode. Weighing 20,000 pounds gross, it can turn in a 15-foot circle and reach a maximum speed of 25 miles per hour. *MFG*

Extreme cold weather operations require that deicing equipment be employed to prepare aircraft for takeoff. An antifreeze fluid is sprayed onto the critical control surfaces, then the aircraft must quickly get off the ground before the surfaces begin to re-freeze. The Stanray Corporation of Vineland, New Jersey, based their 1974 deicer on a unique three-wheel chassis with front steer. A Chrysler 67-horsepower six worked with a single-speed Morse automatic transmission, which hydraulically drove the fluid pump and the drive axle. It had a maneuverable boom-mounted basket for the operator, and carried 1,000 gallons of deicer fluid, 50 gallons of detergent for normal washing, and had an auxiliary engine to heat the deicer fluids. FMC built a similar three-wheel unit for the Navy.

With the introduction of the giant C5A Galaxy cargo aircraft into the air fleet, the ancillary equipment needed to be comparatively larger as well. This 2,500-gallon deicer was mounted on a Calavar Corporation "Condor" chassis and was designated as A/S 32 M-13 by the Air Force. It was 40 feet long, weighed 52,950 pounds gross, and sat on a 210-inch wheelbase. An International Harvester 450-ci gasoline engine worked with an Allison 68-69MT41 transmission, allowing 45 miles per hour, and the FWD chassis had a Timken 38,000 pound rear bogie. The deicing equipment was powered by a Ford 330-ci V-8 with 114 horsepower. The Air Force eventually removed the deicing gear from the M-13s and used the Calavars as 120-foot bucket trucks for routine maintenance.

By 1990, the Air Force had replaced most of the Calavars with this high lift unit, which rides on a chassis built by Special Trucks Incorporated of Fort Wayne, Indiana. STI bases most of their designs on Navistar components, and this one used a series 4900 chassis with STI's own Lo Badger low silhouette cab. The engine is behind the cab and front axle, and the 120-foot boom equipment is by Reach All, with a work basket capable of holding four technicians and lifting 1,500 pounds. The boom consists of six telescoping elements, with a knuckle assembly halfway up from the 360-degree rotating platform.

Since the 1970s, the Air Force has usually opted for deicing units that are based on more practical and cost-effective commercial truck chassis. First there were Dodges, then Ford's excellent C-series formed the basis for the large majority of these newer deicers. The deicing equipment has recently been built by Landoll of Marysville, Kansas. This 1995 Model TM1800 is shown in an elevated mode with the pump operating. The cab roof has a glass panel with wipers, so the operator in the cab can observe the location of the operator in the bucket. Sitting on a compact 135-inch wheelbase, it used a 8.2-liter Cummins diesel, Allison four-speed transmission, and 11.00x20 tires. The deicer had two 1 million btu heaters, and was powered by a Perkins T4.236 diesel. *MFG*

In 1987, the Navy began to replace the 20- to 30-year-old LeTourneau crash cranes used on carrier decks. They were known as Carrier Vessel Crash Crane (CVCC, for jet planes) and the Amphibious Assault Crash Crane (AACC, for helicopters), built by Lake Shore Inc. of Iron Mountain, Michigan. This is the AACC, lifting an F-4 Phantom aboard the U.S.S. *Saipan*. Both cranes can lift about 35 tons 25 feet high, turn in about 30 feet, and move at eight miles per hour. A total of 30 were built, with a 415-horsepower Detroit Diesel 6V-92TA engine powering a 150,000 watt Marathon generator set, which in turn drives the two axles under the boom. The system had only two speeds: idling continually during flight operations, or at full load when moving or lifting. *GP*

The LeTourneau Company continued to build carrier-based mobile cranes well into the 1970s, and this is one of the last models based on the LeTourneau designs. Known as the NS-50, it was an immense unit and was no longer capable of being tucked into some tight corner of the carrier deck as LeTourneau's old C-202 series had been. But true to tradition, the NP-50 still had a diesel engine to drive the generator, then drove each of the four wheels using an electric motor mounted in the wheel. The centrally-mounted winch was also driven electrically, with the controls in the cab being a bank of toggle switches. *NAEC*

Modern Tracked Vehicles

CHAPTER SEVEN

TANKS, ARMORED PERSONNEL CARRIERS, SELF-PROPELLED ARTILLERY, MISSILE CARRIERS, AND ENGINEER EQUIPMENT

Despite their considerable drawbacks, full-tracked vehicles will always have a major role to play in any foreseen military environment. When the weights transported are very heavy, when the ground traversed is less than solid, when recoil from big guns drives the transporter backward every time a round is fired, and as long as there is a threat of running over explosive devices, the undercarriage will probably have tracks.

When moving, a tracked vehicle lays down a roadway for itself that is supposed to lie perfectly still while the vehicle moves over it, but then it is snapped up and returned to the front at twice the speed of the vehicle, thereby creating some formidable forces of movement, and a lot of wear on the track segments.

Tracked chassis, especially those intended for use in the combat zone, can take a lot of punishment. The very weight of a conventional track and its road wheels discourages minor incidents from becoming major problems. True, once a track is blown off, it takes a while to get the vehicle back into operation, but there have been improvements in that area. And ever so slowly, we are moving toward the day when a continuous rubber-coated track will be used on major end items such as personnel carriers and tanks.

Actually, we have had the continuous rubber tracks with us since the early days of World War II. The famous half-track vehicles of that era relied on steel cables encased in rubber, but they were relatively small, working only on the rear of a truck-based vehicle, and the tracks could be manhandled relatively easily. However, it was obvious by the end of the war that the tracks had been quite durable. That some of our allies continued to use those half-tracked vehicles right up into the 1990s did not hurt their reputations either.

The latest version is by Caterpillar and is another edition of the rubber-coated, steel cable concept. Used on their 30/30 "Deuce" engineer vehicle, which is soon to be fielded with the Army, the track system has proven to be nearly indestructible.

Most of America's military tracked vehicles, however, continue today to run on metal tracks, including the tanks, armored personnel carriers, fighting vehicles, and tank recovery vehicles. Along

Cadillac Gage introduced their Stingray light tank in the mid-1980s as a candidate for the proposed Army light divisions. The Stingray is still offered, now weighing 46,750 pounds gross, and it is 30 feet, 6 inches long, with a crew of four. A 105-millimeter low recoil Royal Ordnance gun was fitted into a turret with 360 degrees traverse. The road wheels are suspended by torsion bars and independent trailing arms, and it can move at 45 miles per hour powered by a Detroit Diesel 8V92-TA engine with 550 horsepower. The transmission is an Allison transmission that incorporates the steer unit, and the final drives are planetary with a 4:1 ratio. *MFG*

with the great weight and difficulty in maintaining them, another major problem with tracked vehicles is that the tracks are by nature rather noisy due to the metal-to-metal contact that is inherent in most designs. Tracked vehicles are also relatively slow due both to the initial weight of the vehicle involved, and to the physics of operating a heavy full-length track on each side of the vehicle.

They also tend to have less space available inside the body, or hull, than a comparable wheeled vehicle would have, again thanks to the need to not only lay down a track for the vehicle to run over, but the track must have room alongside the body to return to the front as well.

Along with the tracks themselves, there must be a complex suspension system, and both require

an inordinate amount of maintenance, thanks partially to the types of terrain where tracked vehicles usually operate. In fact, military tracked vehicles generally require an hour of maintenance for every hour of operation, where wheeled tactical vehicles can get by with one hour for every four hours of operation.

Of course, there are many tracked vehicles in the military inventory that are not tanks, APCs, or specialized engineer types. We have tracked tractors for clearing land and grading roadways, and tracked carriers that can move equally well on soft terrain, sand, or in the snow. There are amphibious versions of those tracked carriers, and of course there will always be the lightly armored amphibian landing craft of the Marine Corps.

A right rear view of the M8 AGS from United Defense shows the baffling used behind the engine compartment, and the addition of stand-off supplemental armor encircling the turret and mounted on the sides. The main gun is a 105-millimeter M35 soft recoil unit with an autoloader that can supply 12 rounds per minute, and has 21 ready rounds with nine more outside the loader. A 7.62-millimeter M240 coaxial machine gun is also fitted. Although the program to purchase new light tanks was dismantled several years ago, this M8 was on display at the 1997 Armored Conference at Fort Knox, Kentucky.

When the Army balked at buying the Armored Gun System, the old M551 Sheridans had to keep working. Actually, they performed up to expectations in both Just Cause and in Desert Storm, serving as the Army's only rapidly deployable light armored vehicle. It is also the only tank in the inventory that can be air dropped. There are not many M551s left,

this being one of only 57 owned by the 82nd Airborne Division. It still has its original 152-millimeter main gun, which can fire a Shillelagh missile, high explosive anti-tank round, or a canister round that encases 10,000 steel flechettes. The upgraded M551 has a passive gunner's night vision system sourced from the Bradley, along with a thermal viewer for the tank commander. A large fleet of modified Sheridans also serve at the Army's Desert Training Center as Opposing Force (OPFOR) vehicles. *AD*

Nearly all of the old M60 series tanks are now retired, leaving the M1 and its derivatives as the only medium tank in service in the United States. Upgrades for the M1A1 included a 120-millimeter main gun, blowout panels above the ammunition storage area, and improved NBC protection. Improvements for the M1A2 model included thermal viewers, CO_2 laser rangefinder, a new commander's weapon station, the IVIS communication gear, and a land navigation system. There was also a change from the Chobham sandwich armor used in the original M1 to armor made of depleted uranium, which would increase the weight of an M1A1 to 70 tons v. 58 tons for the normal M1A1. This M1A1 being loaded during Desert Storm has an Auxiliary Power Unit hung on the right rear that will provide power for the turret and radios when the main engine is shut down. *AFCC*

Beginning in 1993, the Army upgraded over 900 M1A1 tanks to the M1A2 configuration, and another 400 to an M1A1D status. The D model had an improved land navigation system, depleted uranium armor, and a databus to provide better interoperability between systems. This is a M1A2, with the cylindrical commander's independent thermal viewer (CITV), which allows a view even through smoke, fog, or night; the driver has a similar night-vision thermal viewer. There was also a new radio interface unit, digital electronics control unit, and enhanced suspension components to handle the increased weight. The 1,500-horsepower gas turbine engine was still used in the new models, with a hydrokinetic transmission with four speeds forward, two in reverse. *MFG*

The M113 series armored personnel carriers (APC) have been in the fleet since the 1960s and have been upgraded as required with diesel engines and better armor and armament. The current types have a Detroit Diesel 6V53T engine with 275 horsepower and an Allison X200-4 hydrokinetic transmission. This version is known as the Mobile Tactical Vehicle Light, (a similar model is marketed as the Combat Engineer Support Vehicle [CESV]), and it features a 350-horsepower 6V53TA engine that is turbocharged and aftercooled, and an improved suspension with 15 inches of roadwheel travel. As shown here, the MTVL also has titanium/steel appliqué armor, and a spaced laminate sheet to protect the floor. The GVW is 36,000 pounds, and it can exceed 50 miles per hour. *MFG*

The M1068A3 is the latest in a long series of command post vehicles built by FMC (now United Defense) based on the old M113 series chassis. It is designed to carry the Army Tactical Command and Control System (ATTCS), and includes improvements in the work areas, along with AC/DC power, a communications distribution system, NBC protection, and a 10-meter telescoping antenna mast. A new 5,000 watt diesel auxiliary power unit uses the main engine's fuel

supply, and can be operated from inside the hull. The GVW is 27,100 pounds combat loaded, and as with all M113 derivatives, it will swim when properly prepared. *MFG*

This experimental M113 by the Army is unique in its field. It is an Advanced Hybrid Electric unit, which has 54 batteries stored in the rear sponsons, a converter in the white box seen inside the hull, and a dual motor drive package at the lower front. A 55 kW gas turbine auxiliary power unit is mounted on the forward hull floor, used to recharge the lead acid batteries, which in turn drive electric motors in the final drives. The driver sits at the upper left of the hull. This electric drive system has been under development since the late 1980s.

The Bradley family of fighting vehicles includes this A2 version with 5.5 tons of add-on armor, bringing the total weight up to 60,000 pounds. To make it even safer, fuel lines were repositioned, ammunition stowage areas relocated, and the Halon fire extinguisher system was improved. A 600-horsepower Cummins VTA-903T diesel engine was fitted, along with a General Electric HMPT-500-3 hydromechanical transmission to handle the extra weight. The latest variant is this M2A3 Infantry Fighting Vehicle, and it has a databus built in, with central processor and mass memory units, and digital information displays for the crew. An improved night sight, and target sighting and tracking capability are also included. The A3 also has a reinforced roof, and fixtures for attaching stand-off armor tiles. *MFG*

The M981 FISTV was a Fire Support Team Vehicle that was based on the M113, and employed a TOW missile launcher that could be depressed for travel. The new version uses United Defense's Bradley chassis, and incorporates an eye-safe laser rangefinder, an improved targeting station control display, and the digital electronic vehicle intercommunications system known as IVIS. As the XM7 Bradley FIST, it also has an inertial navigation system, and an armored TOW missile launcher assembly that pivots up for firing. The secondary weapon is a 25-millimeter Chain Gun automatic cannon. *MFG*

The current training mission for the military requires opposition forces (OPFOR) vehicles, which strongly resemble the enemy's equipment. Since the Berlin Wall fell and Desert Storm ended, numerous items of Czech, East German, and Russian manufacture have been used for training by the Americans, but there is still a need for simulators such as this M113A3/BMP-2 OSV, which is a U.S. M113A3 APC with a superstructure added to make it resemble the Russian BMP-2 personnel carrier. Designed and built at Red River Army Depot in Texas, it will be used at the National Training Center at Fort Irwin, California. *GP*

This is one of the real Russian vehicles currently being used for training in California. Designated as the XM13S, it uses a real MT-LB armored personnel carrier as the chassis. As with the American M113, the Soviet MT-LB served numerous roles with the Russian army including prime mover, command vehicle, ambulance, etc. The training simulators mounted on the XM13S include a surface-to-air missile system and the necessary radar tracking and optical/infrared guidance systems. Although these simulators do not actually fire missiles, they do have sophisticated instrumentation for collecting data. *GP*

Removing casualties from a combat zone will be made somewhat easier with the employment of this Armored Treatment and Transport Vehicle (ATTV) by United Defense. As an armored ambulance, it would improve survivability rates, and it can be configured either as an evacuation unit or as a treatment facility, with 859 cubic feet of space inside the enclosure. The armored hull provides ballistic, environmental, and biochemical protection for the patients. The interior is climate-controlled, and there is an on-board generator to power the medical systems without relying on the big 600-horsepower Cummins VTA-903T main engine. The ATTV is based on the M1108 Universal Carrier. *GP*

SELF-PROPELLED ARTILLERY

The only self-propelled guns currently in use with the U.S. Army fire 155-millimeter rounds. A 1990 howitzer improvement program (HIP) was to upgrade the 1960s M109 self-propelled howitzer to M109A6 specifications. The changes included an integral automatic fire control system, a new cannon with 25-percent increase in range (to about 30,000 meters), and Kevlar inside panels. Hydraulic lines were re-routed for a safer interior, and there was armor to isolate the ammunition from the crew compartment. By the spring of 1991, the new BMY weapon was labeled the Paladin, and the goal was to upgrade more than 800 M109A2s to the A6 configuration until a totally new weapon is fielded in about 2004. *GP*

Another version of the M109A2 upgrade was to be this M109A5 by BMY, which got the improved 155-millimeter cannon and gun mount of the Paladin, but not the extra survivability components. As a less expensive alternative to the Paladin M109A6, it did not have the onboard automatic fire control and navigation systems, which allows the Paladin to stop, take aim, load, shoot, and be on the way again without the crew ever getting out of the vehicle. Those elements however could be added at extra cost. Both the A5 and A6 have upgraded tracks, turret traverse mechanisms, a new 440-horsepower two-cycle diesel engine with low heat rejection feature, a more durable transmission, and an improved elevation/equilibration system. *MFG*

MISSILE CARRIERS

With the celebrated Patriot missile system being trailer-mounted and pulled by trucks, the only tracked missile system in the U.S. fleet is the Multiple-Launch Rocket System (MLRS) by Loral of Dallas, Texas. It was first fielded in 1991, and has become the mainstay artillery rocket system. During the Gulf War, over 180 MLRS launchers were deployed with the Americans, and they fired 9,660 rockets. They were most effective against artillery positions due to the warheads used, which dispersed 644 anti-everything grenades over an area 200 feet in diameter. Depending on how they were aimed, 12 rockets could cover six to 60 acres with nearly 8,000 submunitions. The GVW of the complete vehicle is 28 tons, and a Cummins VTA-903T with 500 horsepower and GE HMPT-500-3 hydromechanical transmission drove the rig. *MFG*

ENGINEER VEHICLES

Initially known as the Counter-Obstacle Vehicle (COV), this United Defense machine has now been redesignated as the Grizzly. It has a giant arm mounted on the right front corner that can reach out 30 feet with its 1.5-cubic-yard bucket. It also has a 14-foot-wide mine clearing blade on the front and external cameras so the operator can see what the machine is doing without being exposed to enemy fire. The Grizzly is based on a M1 tank chassis, and uses the AGT-1500 turbine engine, XM1000 transmission, suspension, and final drive from the M1 series tank. It weighs 70 tons, but can still run close to 50 miles per hour. *MFG*

General Dynamics and MAN GHH of Germany have teamed up to build this Wolverine heavy assault bridge (HAB). It is to be the replacement for the aging AVLB, which is based on the M60 series medium tank. It differs from the earlier types in that they were a scissors design (hinged in the middle), while the Wolverine uses an auxiliary diesel engine to first slide the lower section out, then the second section drops and is coupled to the first section, and the entire 85-foot bridge assembly is moved out to the front without touching the ground until it is ready to emplace. The aluminum bridge weighs 12 tons, while the complete vehicle is 70 tons. It can launch a bridge in five minutes and retrieve one in 10 minutes. Based on a M1 tank chassis, it uses the normal AGT-1500 engine and a X1100 transmission. *MFG*

Hard at work in the Persian Gulf during Desert Storm is a c.1987 Fiat-Allis Model 14C. It belonged to the Air Force, and curiously lacked any rollover protection or even a sun shade. The olive paint job is the only variance from a civilian version, and it used Fiat's 168-horsepower Model 8365T six-cylinder turbocharged diesel with 494 cid, a powershift torque converter transmission with three speeds forward and reverse, and double reduction final drives. Steering was via multiple disc, oil-cooled clutches, and a gear type hydraulic pump operated the 10-foot 4-inch blade. *AFCC*

This Caterpillar D7G has been equipped to satisfy the most demanding soldier-operator. They were used in Desert Storm by all services, and they feature a 638-cid Caterpillar Model 3306T diesel of 200 horsepower, a planetary powershift torque converter transmission with three speeds forward and reverse, and hydraulic, oil-cooled multiple disc clutch steering. Weighing more than 45,000 pounds with the Model 57 winch at the rear, it has a substantial cab, which can even be air conditioned. Special changes for military use include electromagnetic radiation suppression, a coating to resist chemical agents, slave receptacle, and a STA-ICE (trouble diagnosis) system. *MFG*

Clearly the ultimate in militarized bulldozers, this is another Caterpillar D7G, but this one is equipped to walk through land mines. Editions of this served in the Persian Gulf and have recently gone to Bosnia as well. It carries the Mine Clearing/Armor Protection (MCAP) kit, similar to those kept in readiness for early reaction forces. The cab is made of 1/2-inch rolled homogeneous armor, and similar protection is provided for engine, radiator, hydraulic lines, fuel tanks and batteries. MCAP kits are available for the big D8N tractor, the 320L Hydraulic Excavator, and for the 963 Track-type Loader. *MFG*

With its 116-inch-wide blade buried deep in the soil, the Army's new Deployable Universal Combat Earthmover (DEUCE) leaves a deep impression wherever it goes. Built by Caterpillar, it is a fascinating machine, which weighs 34,500 pounds gross. The rubber tracks are unique, offering both speed and reduced maintenance. It is a "two mode" machine, selectable by a switch. The "self-deployable" mode has 265 horsepower, a fully automatic transmission with six speeds forward, a hydropneumatic suspension with 10 inches of vertical travel for the road wheels while moving at 30 miles per hour, and the dozer blade locked up. In the "earthmoving" mode, it has 185 horsepower available, a three-speed powershift transmission, 7.3-miles-per-hour maximum speed, a rigid suspension, and working blade. *MFG*

The engine for the Deuce (earlier known as the 30/30) is Caterpillar's 3126 diesel, and the transmission is their planetary powershift. The drawbar pull is 25,000 pounds at one mile per hour in the earthmoving mode. The cab tilts

forward for maintenance access to the engine, and it is air conditioned and heated. To simplify training, the Deuce has normal automotive controls: steering wheel, accelerator and brake pedals, instead of lateral levers. The suspension can be lowered for increased clearance in an aircraft, and it can be prepared for airlift in 10 minutes, for air drop in less than 20 minutes. Production of the Deuce began in the spring of 1997, and eventually the Army plans to have a total of 184. *MFG*

CHAPTER EIGHT

SPECIALIZED TRACKED VEHICLES

There are three basic types of tracked equipment included in this chapter: a recovery vehicle designed to retrieve disabled tanks, the Navy's tracked landing vehicles, and general purpose commercial carriers.

The only new recovery vehicle in the Army's inventory today is the updated M88A2, but it derives from a long line of specialized vehicles dating back to World War II. Most of the early ones were based on modification of tanks that were then in service, meaning that there were numerous interchangeable parts. However, as tanks grew in size, it became more difficult for a similar-size vehicle to effectively pull them out of the mud or to put them upright when they had rolled over, so it was necessary to build tracked recovery vehicles just for that purpose. The M88 series was introduced in the early 1960s, and the current edition is quite similar in appearance, but has considerably more power, lifting, and pulling ability.

The tracked landing vehicles (LVT) also have a remarkable history, considering the initial model was developed more than 60 years ago as a civilian rescue craft for work in the Florida Everglades. There have been more than 100 variants on the LVT since its inception, and the models found in the Marine Corps' fleet today are as unique as their predecessors in that they can carry troops and supplies through the open ocean, across the surf, up onto the beach, and keep moving inland as required.

Throughout World War II, LVTs relied on tracks for propulsion in the water, with water jets being added to LVTP7 models of the 1960s and bringing the water speed up to around 7 miles per hour. The version now being evaluated will have an aquaplaning system, which will lift the hull out of the water on the open ocean, allowing water speeds of 30 miles per hour.

The current range of cargo carriers includes lightweight snow machines, which are similar in design to the grooming equipment found on ski slopes, but they will usually have a cargo/crew compartment to carry 4 to 10 people. At the heavy end of the carrier line are the armored vehicles, which will usually be found as transporters for communications and electronics equipment on the battlefield, and for carrying ammunition in support of tracked self-propelled artillery weapons.

The Marine Corps are the sole users of LVTs, and they have an illustrious history going back to 1935 when Donald Roebling built an aluminum amphibian to help rescue stranded survivors of Florida storms. He called his tractor the Alligator, and by 1941, the Navy had purchased 150 of them. They were indispensable during World War II, ferrying troops and equipment from the mother ships right up across the beaches and on inland. The Navy has developed these LVTs to a fine art over the years, and the modern successors will often have armor protection, as does this AAV7A1 in Saudi Arabia. The Block I appliqué armor seen here is intended to defeat rocket-propelled grenades and high-explosive anti-tank (HEAT) rounds. *AFCC*

RECOVERY VEHICLES

The only tracked recovery vehicle (VTR) currently in the military fleet is this M88A2. Now known as the Hercules, it was known developmentally as the M88A1E1. It has an improved Teledyne Continental AVDS-1790-8DR engine that delivers a full 1,050 horsepower, and works with an Allison XT-1410-5A transmission. It has improved, power-assisted brakes, and can easily recover the M1A2 medium tank using its 70-ton-capacity front winch. The elevated rectangular section boom can lift 35 tons (v. 25 tons for the M88A1), and the towing capacity is 70 tons (v. 56 tons for the M88A1). It has a 6,000-pound lead winch to help deploy the main winch cable, which is 280 feet long. It has new overlay armor around the crew compartment, and ballistic skirts to help protect the tracks and suspension system.

LANDING VEHICLES TRACKED (LVT)

The FMC-built AAV7A1 is a continuation of the LVTP7A1, first introduced in 1984. There are several versions, including a personnel carrier (AAVP7A1), command vehicle (AAVC7A1), and a recovery type (AAVR7A1). They can move through 10-foot swells along the beach, powered by a 400-horsepower Cummins multifuel Model VT400, which is a water-cooled, turbocharged V-8, and has a NAVSEA HS400-3A1 transmission with hydraulic lockup torque converter. It moves in the water by a 14,000-gallons-per-minute water jet, and by spinning the tracks. This is an AAVP7A1 that served with the Marines in Desert Storm, and it shows the trim vane hinged out of the way under the nose. *AFCC*

The latest LVT offering for the Marine Corps' fleet is this General Dynamics' Advanced Amphibious Assault Vehicle (AAAV). Although not yet approved for purchase, it meets the Navy's requirements for an amphibious landing craft well into the 2000s. It is driven by two 23-inch water jets, and with a large trim vane in place and the road wheels retracted, it can reach 30 miles per hour aquaplaning in the water. On land it will run 45 miles per hour. With an aluminum alloy hull, the GVW is 70,925 pounds, with the crew of three and 18 combat troops aboard. The engine is a MTU Model MT883K-523 diesel, with 2,600 horsepower in the water mode, 800 horsepower in the land mode. An Allison X300 transmission powers the water jets or tracks. The primary weapon is a 25-millimeter M242 Bushmaster, and the coaxial machine gun is a 7.62 M240. *MFG*

Tracked carriers range from relatively lightweight machines such as this Bombardier Skidozer 252D to totally armored combat vehicles. The 252D is intended primarily for cold weather operations, and the Air Force has many of them working in Greenland, where this one is assigned to Kulusuk Air Station. The tracks are over 3 feet wide, giving excellent performance on soft snow, and the power is via a six-cylinder Ford engine of 132 horsepower, working with a Ford C6 three-speed automatic transmission. A planetary controlled differential is used, and this provides steering and stopping by controlling the tracks. It has pneumatic tires, and each axle is suspended by a torsion bar. Although it weighs more than 5 tons loaded, it can move at 35 miles per hour and climb an 80-percent grade.

The Army owns several examples of this Model LMC 3700C, built by the Logan Manufacturing Company. They are used in Alaska to groom slopes, and to pull lines of soldiers on skis during training operations. The 10-way blade at the front

can cut through snow drifts and groom the snow, while the 57-inch-wide tracks help to pack the snow. The engine is a Caterpillar 3208T turbocharged diesel with 250 horsepower at 2,800 rpm, and the hydrostatic transmission consists of two-speed Sundstrand hydraulic motors working with two Sundstrand hydraulic pumps that power the tracks and provide the brakes. Net weight is 11,400 pounds, top speed is 10 miles per hour, and it can climb a 100-percent slope, or run on a 75-percent side slope. A winch is fitted just behind the 60-gallon fuel tank. *MFG*

In the late 1980s, LMC built a series of their Model 1500 for the Army, Navy, and Air Force in at least three variations: two-man pickup, five-man crew cab with small pickup body (seen here), or as a full length cargo/passenger carrier. A protective roll cage was included with each type, and this one has a protective cover over the cargo bed. An Army 1500 is pictured here with the 28-inch-wide summer tracks; winter tracks were 36 inches wide, and it weighed 4,800 pounds net with the heavier tracks. They could climb a 90-percent grade on dirt or packed snow, 75 percent on soft snow. An AMC six-cylinder gasoline engine with 120 horsepower from 258 cubic inches was used, along with a Chrysler A727 three-speed automatic transmission and a planetary controlled differential. There were four 4.50x12 pneumatic tires on each side, plus the drive sprocket. *MFG*

At the other extreme from the light, nimble snow tractors is this quite heavy and armored XM1108 Universal Carrier, built by United Defense (FMC/BMY). It is based on M113A3 components, including Detroit Diesel's 6V53T engine with 350 horsepower from 318 ci displacement, and an Allison X200-4A hydrokinetic transmission that does the braking and steering. It uses torsion bars for the six (per side) road wheels, and there is 9 inches of vertical travel for each road wheel. The GVW of the XM1108 is 36,000 pounds, with 15,000 being payload. *MFG*

A United Defense M993 chassis is seen here with the XM4 Command and Control Vehicle (C2V) module installed. Based on components from the M2/M3 Bradley vehicles, it has numerous antennae to support the radios and other communications gear inside the shelter, and it also has biological and chemical protection, and environmental controls as well. It weighs from 56,000 to 66,000 pounds when fully equipped. Power is via a Cummins VTA-903T four-cycle diesel, with 600 horsepower, and this drives a General Electric HMPT500-3EC hydromechanical transmission with hydrostatic steering and brakes. The enclosure has its own Cummins 6BT5.9 diesel, operating the AC and DC generators. *GP*

Originally built by BMY as the M992 FAASV, this is the Field Artillery Ammunition Support Vehicle, and it works closely with the M109A6 Paladin discussed earlier. When backed up to the Paladin, this M992A2 can feed in 90 rounds of 155 ammunition, which are stored in racks inside the hull. A conveyor system moves the rounds directly into the M109A6, and it is all protected by an armored superstructure. A global positioning system (GPS) or an inertial navigation system (INS) can be included. The M992A2 can also serve as a prime mover for towed artillery, and it has an auxiliary power unit (APU) to support other equipment. This one is laboring through the Saudi Arabian desert after a heavy rain. *SS*

The M992A2 vehicle can also be configured as an artillery fire direction center (FDCV) or as a command post vehicle (CPV). With a 750-cubic-foot interior and enough height so the average person can stand straight, it can accommodate nine operators plus the driver. The interior is able to handle current computer-based information management systems, and it can be built with fire suppression and NBC protection systems as well. The engine for these newer A2 models is a Detroit Diesel 8V71LHR with 440 horsepower, and the transmission is an Allison cross-drive XTG-411-4 with four forward speeds. *MFG*

INDEX